Evol to Succeed

THE ENTREPRENEUR'S JOURNEY

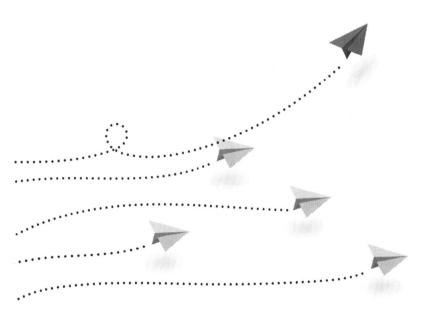

WARREN MUNSON

ISBN: 9781794289086

Independently published by Amazon KDP

Copyright Warren Munson 2019.

For further information, please contact info@inspire.uk.net

This work was produced in collaboration with Write Business Results Ltd. For more information on Write Business Results' business book services, please visit our website:

www.writebusinessresults.com or contact us on: 020 3752 7057 or info@writebusinessresults.com

 WRITE BUSINESS RESULTS

Contents

Introduction

In 2014, Inspire, an entrepreneurial accountancy business, celebrated its tenth anniversary. It had successfully navigated from the startup phase and was growing in size and revenues... but something wasn't right. The founder had lost all joy for his work, and the company was taking on business from wherever it came. The original passion and belief of the startup phase, and the focus on just one important segment of the market – serving entrepreneurial businesses – had been lost. As a result, the founder and the company were heading for a slow decline into failure; what I call falling into the 'valley of despair'. Luckily, using the techniques that I'm going to discuss in this book, this situation was reversed and the company was able to remain successful while getting back to its core values and embracing what made it unique.

And who was the founder who led Inspire through all this? It was me, Warren Munson. Using this experience, and what I've seen from working with hundreds of entrepreneurs, this book will guide entrepreneurs through the minefield of early success in order to build a solid foundation for a strong, scalable business that can move into the future with purpose and positivity.

WHO IS THIS BOOK FOR?

'Entrepreneur' is a term that's become widely used in the past few years: to some it will seem like it's a word that only applies to people who go on Dragon's Den. In this book, however, I'm using it to mean individuals who might describe themselves as owner-managers, self-employed shareholders, directors, or founders. Whichever of these titles you might have taken, if you are ambitious and driven, and are on a journey to grow and scale your business, for me you're an entrepreneur and this book is for you.

There are lots of different types of entrepreneur, and it will be useful when reading this book to figure out which you are. The four main types – though there are more – are as follows: the first is the innovating entrepreneur, who sees a new piece of technology, a new way to develop a product, or a new way to be disruptive in their industry; they start their business and their journey to innovate and to create new products and services – James Dyson is a great example of this. The second is the inspirational or visionary entrepreneur, such as Richard Branson: they have the ability to think and see things differently, and spot and seize opportunities. The third is the evolutionary entrepreneur, who often starts up their business because that's the typical thing to do in their industry; over time they may well move onto creating something larger, diversifying and going on their entrepreneurial journey. And the final category is the circumstantial entrepreneur: these may have inherited a family business, bought a pre-existing business or have become a business owner as some other consequence of circumstance; in this case it's this event that activates entrepreneurial spirit and encourages them to take the business forward.

On top of that, the book has a lot of advice for entrepreneurs who have achieved some initial success, and especially those who are beginning to experience any first feelings of disillusionment. Almost every entrepreneur will go through this, and this book will help to guide you through these feelings and return your focus to your core drive, so that those initial successes grow into grand scale triumphant victories later on. The simple principle is you need to evolve to succeed.

STRUCTURE OF THE BOOK

The book has been divided into five chapters – let's briefly look now at what each chapter will cover.

CHAPTER 1: THE ENTREPRENEURIAL JOURNEY

Most entrepreneurs in the first few years of their business will experience similar journeys. In this chapter I'll explore what this journey normally looks like in detail, comparing it against what happened with my own story and Inspire. We'll also look at some of the pitfalls and danger signs that you can come across on the journey.

CHAPTER 2: AMBITION, ESSENCE, SPIRIT AND BELIEFS

When starting a business it's often quite clear to the entrepreneur why they're embarking on this journey and the values they want the business to embody: these are the ambition, essence, spirit and beliefs of the business. Sometimes these core elements can be lost along the way while focusing too heavily on profits and growth: this chapter will help you clearly define them, and find your way back to them if the business has strayed.

CHAPTER 3: PERSONAL DEVELOPMENT

As an entrepreneur it's important to be a strong leader and have the skills necessary to take the business where it needs to go. That's why personal development is so key: all the skills necessary to do well can be trained, and almost no entrepreneurs are talented in all of them innately. As you move forward and your business grows, it's necessary to also grow your skillset and the skillset of your team so that you can continue to scale and grow the business.

CHAPTER 4: BUSINESS FUNDAMENTALS

This is the most practical chapter in the book. I'll cover principles for running your business well, including recruiting and retaining a stellar team, having great financials and reporting, and explain why I don't recommend specific business models when entrepreneurial businesses are by their nature very unique.

CHAPTER 5: THE FUTURE

The final chapter focuses on the future of your business. Entrepreneurs often get caught up in the day-to-day of running things and forget about future development: it's important for them to be looking for future threats and opportunities, and to be thinking about and building towards the long-term value of their business. As the leader of the company this is entirely your responsibility, and this chapter will help you discover how best to go about it.

Now, let's dive straight into the entrepreneurial journey with Chapter 1.

CHAPTER I

The Entrepreneurial Journey

There is a fairly typical journey in the entrepreneurial world which many business owners will go through as their company grows. I am not talking about what 'should' happen, or what inevitably happens to everyone, but it is a very common story. This journey moves from the initial startup phase filled with energy and vision, through a success and growth phase, and then via that growth into what I call the 'valley of despair'. This stage can be a slow business killer, draining the entrepreneur and bogging them down in the various changing pressures of a young business that has achieved success.

In this chapter I'll go into detail about the typical entrepreneur's journey and discuss some of the difficulties of running a business at its midpoint in growth, as well as delving into my own personal story which followed this path quite closely. The idea behind this is to help identify whether you're heading for the valley of despair – or indeed whether you're already there – and to share valuable advice along the way to avoid or rectify this situation. Let's begin by looking at the startup phase.

Enabling you to Succeed

Your journey as an entrepreneur follows a path which, while unique
and personal to you, will take you through the stages below:

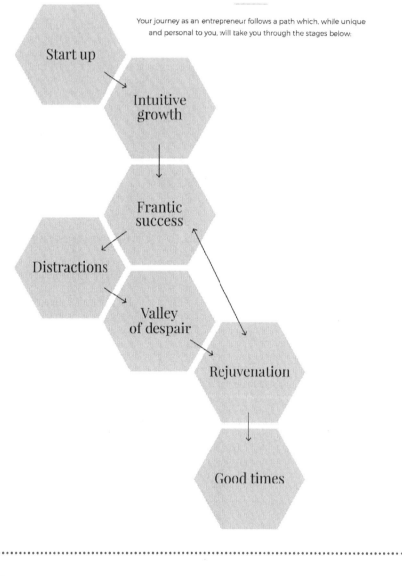

Start up

Intuitive growth

Frantic success

Distractions

Valley of despair

Rejuvenation

Good times

THE ENTREPRENEUR'S JOURNEY

STARTUP PHASE

Most entrepreneurs begin their business with a real sense of meaning and purpose. They know what they want their business to be about, they are focused and believe in what they're doing, and they are passionate about making a difference. This is because almost every successful business begins with a strong 'why' which has nothing to do with making money. This could be that they want to deliver better customer service than anyone in the industry, or to make the world a better place, or to create something truly innovative.

Of course there are some business owners out there who started out to simply do their job working for themselves. But this book is aimed specifically at those who want to create a truly scalable business which makes a difference. With these entrepreneurs the startup phase is defined by high energy and a real buzz. The small team really believes in what they are doing, which gets them through the tough times and long hours of the startup phase. Come what may, they're prepared to jump any hurdle, knock down any barrier and go the extra mile to achieve their goals because they have such a strong sense of purpose. Very few businesses have quick and easy success, but still everyone is happy and enjoying it, and there's no need to discuss the values that drive the business because everyone just gets it.

WARREN'S STORY 1: FIRST STEPS

At 16 I left education for the world of work. I had a gift for maths so joined a local accountancy firm, and over time trained in sales with the company. After that I spent ten years working in various small, independent firms – but my inner entrepreneur felt stifled. I believed that if I wanted to make a difference, I needed to be somewhere bigger. Somewhere that would allow me to spread my wings and fulfil my potential. I was hungry and ambitious, and it felt like nothing could stop me.

Having fully qualified I was offered a position at a leading national accountancy firm in 1999; I felt like I'd made it. Here was an opportunity to climb the ladder right up to the top rung: partnership. Amazingly, it didn't take long to be offered a number of promotions, and at the age of 30 I found myself in front of the top dogs in reach of the golden ticket. I was to be one of the youngest people ever to be offered partnership, but guess what? I didn't want it. The money was there. The status was there. But I felt that it just wasn't me. I didn't want to become an institutionalised corporate animal.

They didn't let me go easily. In fact, they sent me around the country to meet people who had been made partner. They thought that by seeing how 'happy' and rich they were, I'd change my mind. But it just served to confirm my suspicions of corporate life; those in their late 30s were enjoying the perks; those in their 40s were jaded; and those in their 50s were thinking, 'What have I done with my life?'

I knew that to sidestep the clutches of the corporate world, I needed to jump ship and build my own business. So I handed in my notice and said, 'Whatever you say, whatever you do, I'm sorry but I've just got to do this.' And with their mouths wide open, they watched me walk out of the office empty handed, but full of excitement for my future. I had a loving wife, by now a baby on the way, and now I was about to fulfil my dream of owning my own business.

It was on 5 July 2004 that I officially launched Inspire, an independent accountancy firm dedicated to enabling the entrepreneur to succeed. I felt truly liberated. I was finally in control of my own destiny, or so I thought, doing what I wanted to do. I could make my own choices and be the person I wanted to be.

I started off where most people start off – by myself in a tiny office with a laptop, phone and a desk. But despite my modest surroundings, my vision was ambitious: I would grow a company with meaningful principles and beliefs, and nurture a team that felt truly valued, treating them as individuals.

Sat in that little office, I knew there was a whole world of opportunity before me and I couldn't wait to get stuck in.

A successful startup period means that the business will begin to grow and evolve. Rather than making things easier, this phase is defined by bigger and harder challenges. The hurdles become more like high-jumps, and work-life balance can take a hit. The challenges can be about local client service and delivery, evolution and development of products and services, employee engagement, communication, finding funding, dealing with regulation and red tape, recruitment, or many other things. But underlying all this is still that sense of focused passion and belief, and that's what continues to drive everyone.

WARREN'S STORY 2: THRIVING

A couple of months later I took on my first employee, Sally, to focus on sales and marketing. Then, in November I employed Inspire's first accountant. Things were growing quickly and, with the support of the people around me, I could feel myself catapulting into the marketplace. When my beautiful daughter, Alex, was born in January 2005, I was in the midst of our first significant transaction.

The business continued to grow rapidly, and by the end of the first year we had six employees in the team and the energy and ambition was electric. The firm's growth curve reflected this thirst to succeed; we turned over £150k in year one and £500k in year two. Suffice to say we soon outgrew our offices, so decided to up sticks and move to a larger space in a beautiful rural setting.

We had a shared mission to support entrepreneurs, and we did so with gusto. My personal goal as the business owner was to make Inspire credible and sustainable so that it could continue one day without me. I wanted to create a legacy and brand I could be proud of, and it felt as though I was on the right road to doing so.

INTUITIVE GROWTH AND FRANTIC SUCCESS

Many entrepreneurs find that the next stages of growth, the choices they make and the steps that they take are intuitive. They go with their gut instincts and often – given they've already managed to get to this stage – these lead to success. Customers are attracted to the business because it does things differently to corporate competition or complacent competitors, and as more and more customers come in tasks such as putting processes and systems in place come naturally and intuitively.

However, there is a danger here. In this phase there are many potential lessons to learn that will be essential in the future of the business, but quite often entrepreneurs can be so motivated and excited that they go forward gung-ho, all guns blazing without taking the time to reflect on what is happening. Without reflection, and working solely on intuition, all the possible lessons that could have been learned will go to waste. And with everyone's heads down focusing solely on just getting the job done, the fantastic startup mentality will become diluted and fade. We call this frantic success.

No matter how busy it gets in this period, the entrepreneur must take time out to really think about what is happening and how to adapt, learn, and avoid pitfalls in the future. Otherwise over time their focus may gradually erode, the success may stop and then they won't know how to fix their business. But even if this doesn't happen and the business continues to enjoy success, a frantic period without reflection can lay the groundwork for ending up in the valley of despair later on.

WARREN'S STORY 3: FIRST BRICK WALL

It turns out that pride comes before a fall, and whilst I was busy networking and winning great clients, the firm was not best equipped to deal with the influx of work. By early 2007 the team had grown to 10 members of staff, yet we had no systems or processes, no management structure, and dwindling office morale.

Pressures on the business increased: we were growing by over 30% year-on-year, the dynamic of the team changed and the common goal that had kept us on the same path had become diluted. It was clear that the business needed to grow up. Recognising that we needed more space, I decided to bite the bullet and make a big investment, moving the team to Poole, to our current offices, in May 2007.

We'd survived off youthful energy and ambition up until this point, but with some larger clients coming in and more complex assignments being won, we now needed to make big improvements to our way of working. We had to invest in new IT systems, create a solid management structure, improve our processes and – most importantly – I needed to step up and develop my own skills.

THE DANGER ZONE

At some point the entrepreneur will begin to feel like they're "living the dream". The business has expanded and has momentum, growth and a larger team, and everything seems to be clicking into place. But this is actually the danger zone, which if not careful can lead to the valley of despair.

As each business and individual entrepreneur are unique there are many reasons why a business and an individual can find themselves in the danger zone but the two most common are set out below.

The first is that suddenly the expectation for the business has changed: as a startup it was all about the passion for the business, but now the entrepreneur feels like they have to make a significant profit. It's no longer solely about the vision, but also about paying bills and salaries, adding a new dynamic of pressure to the business. This means that almost inevitably there is a shift in focus away from the original purpose, values and ideals of the startup towards a new guiding light: the pursuit of money.

This shift in focus can mean that the entrepreneur is no longer properly looking after their people: they feel they have to cut corners in systems and processes to save money; their personal motivation is dropping; they're feeling the stress and pressure to make money and this drains their spirit and the energy they were formerly bringing to the office. This is the valley of despair.

The second possible reason is that with success and feeling like they're living the dream, some entrepreneurs begin to believe their own hype. And when they believe that everything they touch will succeed, arrogance creeps in and they become distracted. Their precision levels drop and the business begins to have some failures – they don't know how to deal with these because it goes against their belief that they can do no wrong. The team becomes dispirited and begins to lose faith in the entrepreneur, and the business gradually begins to unravel. This is the alternate version of the valley of despair.

WARREN'S STORY 4: THE LOWEST POINT

At this point, although we were winning business and bringing in a significant number of new clients, it was the wrong type of business. Inspire was founded on a passion for advising and nurturing entrepreneurs, but for a period of time we were saying yes to every opportunity that came our way, without staying true to our niche clientele. On reflection, we were becoming a 'corporate' – we were believing our own hype and becoming everything I didn't want to be.

What broke my heart was that the change had a massive impact on my long-standing team, some of whom handed in their notice saying, 'This is not the Inspire way.' This was a dagger to my heart. I also believe that we started to focus on the money rather than believing in what we were doing and putting our team and clients first.

In 2014, Inspire hosted its 10th anniversary celebration at Bournemouth's O2 Academy. With over 200 invitees, this was a massive event dedicated to saying a big thank you to our staff and clients. If you were to ask any of our guests that night what they thought I was feeling, they'd probably say I was on top of the world. But, believe it or not, the weeks leading up to the event were the lowest moments of my entrepreneurial journey. So low, in fact, that the night before the party I turned to my wife Michala and jokingly said, 'What would you do and what would you say if I stood up on that stage and said I was jacking it all in?'

From the outside looking in, it would be hard to understand why I was at rock bottom amidst all this celebration and success, but the truth of the matter was this: Inspire had lost its USPs. It no longer felt like an innovative, exciting firm that would appeal to entrepreneurs. And I no longer felt inspired. I had turned into the exact thing I'd run away from when I declined partnership back in 2004. I was becoming the corporate man!

But on the evening of the party, the warmth and energy in the room from staff, clients and supporters overwhelmed me. I heard tales of how Inspire helped clients to overcome challenges, stories of where my team had gone the extra mile, and I saw that despite my fears, Inspire was still inspiring people. I can't tell you how much this impacted my state of mind. It saved me, gave me the motivation to carry on, and reaffirmed my belief that so much could still be achieved.

THE VALLEY OF DESPAIR

For many young businesses hitting the valley of despair is the moment of truth. It is possible to recover and escape, but those which don't usually plateau and gradually slide away from what they could have achieved. It's rarely the case that the valley of despair causes a big doomsday collapse of the business, but equally growth will be permanently stunted and results poor. The worst case scenario for the entrepreneur is that they end up feeling like they're trapped in a job they don't really want just to keep the lights on and the doors open; they feel like they might as well be in a job in the corporate world.

REJUVENATION

Escaping, then, is clearly more appealing. I'll explore how to escape the valley of despair throughout this book, but the key strategies are to reflect, reevaluate and reinvent the business to get back to the core purpose and values of the startup phase, and to bring the entrepreneur back to a place of joy.

The best option of all is – naturally – to avoid ever reaching this phase. Some entrepreneurs reading this book may not yet have reached the valley of despair, and for them it may be possible to avoid it entirely. Again, I'll explore more strategies and principles to ensure that you are keeping sight of the big picture in order to spot these kinds of issues coming and evade them. You will then be able to continue with great momentum for the next evolution in the betterment of the business.

WARREN'S STORY 5:
STRIPPING EVERYTHING BACK

With more and more staff expressing their dissatisfaction, and with clients also noticing a dip in service quality, it was clear to me then that something drastic needed to change: everything needed to be stripped back. Really, I needed to transport myself back to the beginning and the feelings I'd had when I started with my simple laptop, phone and desk. In short, I needed to regain my original focus, passion and belief.

So I took my foot off the growth pedal, and exited clients that were not in our niche market and also the more corporate members of staff who did not share Inspire's principles, including one shareholder. I refocused on the reasons I created Inspire in the first place: enabling ambitious entrepreneurs to succeed; nurturing staff; and creating a culture of innovation, enthusiasm and energy. It was tough, but I wish I had been brave and strong enough to make the required changes earlier.

If you think about why you started your business, there will be some founding principles that defined what you wanted to achieve and the manner in which you were going to achieve them. That was my starting point; I knew I needed to create and maintain core values that would guide every element of the business. So I created Inspire's ambition, essence, spirit and beliefs, which soon became the lighthouse by which we navigated.

Today, these principles are as strong as ever, and I don't know where we'd be without them. In summary, our 'Ambition' is our purpose, our

'Essence' is what we do, our 'Spirit' is our energy and emotion and our 'Beliefs' are the guiding principles we follow. They're similar maybe to Vision, Mission and Values, but in my opinion they're far more relevant to an entrepreneurial business.

It took 18 months to change the business and get Inspire's unique culture back, but every second was worth it. We stopped focusing on the competition; we injected the fun back into the office; and we rebuilt a team of like-minded professionals that valued our ambition, essence, spirit and beliefs.

GOOD TIMES

What are 'good times'? This essentially means success, and to a degree it depends on the individual and what success looks like for them. Good times includes both business and personal aspects, so let's look at how to define success in both of these now.

On the business side I use nine broad categories to pinpoint where you are on your entrepreneurial journey, and whether your business is experiencing good times. These are as follows:

- Good work / life balance

- Effective leadership team in place

- In great physical and mental health, low levels of stress

- Systems and processes in place enabling growth

- Cash generation in the business is strong

- Great culture in line with the ambition, essence, spirit and beliefs of the business

- Fantastic team engagement

- Customers and clients love you

- Your personal focus, passion and beliefs are strong and aligned with those you had when you began your entrepreneurial journey

Now take the time to review this list and score each out of 10.

If all these categories have high scores, a lot of business value will be generated. The valuation of a business during good times will be significantly higher, and could allow a lucrative exit if desired.

In the same vein, a business in 'good times' will be well run by a senior management team, giving the owners time to enjoy life, pursue other opportunities, extract funds to create personal wealth etc.

On the personal side, good times mean that you score highly against a list of things in your life which are important to you. It's key to create a list that is honest and accurate, so that you can effectively judge whether you are experiencing success in areas that matter. We'll look at this in more detail and perform an exercise to build and score your list in Chapter 2.

IT'S NOT A LINEAR JOURNEY

From what you've seen in the chapter so far you'd be forgiven for assuming that the entrepreneurial journey is a linear one, from startup, to intuitive growth, frantic success, distractions, the valley of despair, through to rejuvenation and finally ending with good times. But in reality this is rarely the case. Very few of us will simply go through all these stages and be finished with the business. My own personal experience – and that of the many entrepreneurs I've worked with – shows that actually rejuvenation is rarely the end. New ideas are formed, new entrepreneurial challenges attempted, new business opportunities are seized, and the journey begins again, often diving straight back into frantic success. This almost inevitably leads to further distractions, another trip to the valley of despair, and more rejuvenation.

The most savvy entrepreneurs out there, however, by following the tips and tricks in this book, will be able to jump from rejuvenation into frantic success and then straight back to rejuvenation, bouncing between these two states as their business grows, thereby avoiding distractions and the valley of despair. Eventually through this process they will achieve their definition of good times, both personally and from a business perspective.

Realising that this is not a wholly linear process will make it easier for you to recognise where you are on your journey, seize the moment at the right times, and make the most of any opportunity that presents itself.

SUCCESS OVER TIME

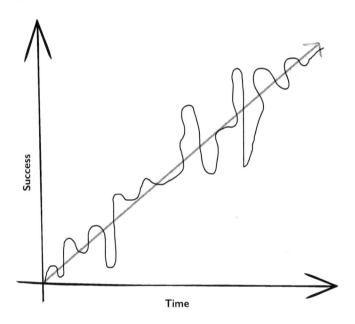

∼∼∼ Purported / typical academic linear journey to success
—— More accurate representation of journey

CONCLUSION

When starting out in a new business entrepreneurs often worry about the external factors which might cause their business to fail. That they may have chosen the wrong product or service at the wrong time and in the wrong place. But the truth is that the majority of businesses which fail within the first three years do so because of internal issues. It's much more common that poor choices in managing the business, or the entrepreneur realising that they don't have enough passion to get them through the tough initial stages, steer the direction of a startup towards failure.

It's very important, then, to keep a close eye on how your business is doing and where it's going, and not just focus on the external market, environment, competition etc. Take a timeout regularly from the day-to-day work of the business to reflect, reevaluate and reassess. Make sure that you are in touch with the original ambition, purpose and passion of the startup phase and try to continue to align the business with those. By doing this it is very possible to avoid the 'typical' journey and never find yourself in the valley of despair, or to escape it if your business is already there.

CHAPTER KEY QUESTIONS AND EXERCISES

Key questions and exercises that you should consider from this chapter are:

- Where are you on your entrepreneurial journey?

- What do you need to do right now to rejuvenate your business and personal energy?

- Score each of the key questions in relation to 'Good Times' out of 10. Where are you strong and weak and where do you need to focus?

- What do good times mean for you and your business?

CHAPTER 2

Ambition, Essence, Spirit and Beliefs

In the previous chapter I discussed the entrepreneurial journey and where you are on that journey. But, no matter what stage you are at, I strongly believe that it's important for you to recognize the personal values that mean a lot to you and to have a strong sense of purpose in the business that you own and operate.

The reason for this is that, while we all begin our journey with a unique sense of passion, focus and belief which serves us well in the early days, over time this often begins to fade, diluted by the growing number of new team members. Unless we set a guiding star against which those in the business can navigate, against which we can recruit new team members, against which we can make contextual decisions about what business we want to take on and how the business should evolve, then we'll find ourselves in difficulties. We become distracted, not aligning ourselves with why we actually started the business, what ignited our passion, or where we found the focus and belief to get the journey under way.

...   In this chapter I'll look at the different elements that should be included in your business's guiding principles, and I would strongly encourage you to write them down and ensure they become part of the culture in every aspect of the business. In the corporate world it's common to have a 'vision, mission and values statement', but these are simply words that come down from distant board members to be written on an office wall, and often the true culture and behaviour of team members has no correlation to the statement. This shouldn't just be an exercise in stating how you'd like your business to be, but rather an ongoing effort to ensure that the business and team members are consistently guided by the principles agreed and demonstrated by the behaviours in the business.

ESTABLISHING PERSONAL FOCUS

Having stated that it's important that your business and your team members are guided by your personal principles, how do we go about establishing what your principles are all about – and significantly what is personally important to you? How do we understand what is really important to you in your life, and thereby gauge and manage success? Answering these questions is the first step towards understanding and establishing the business's ambition, essence, spirit and beliefs.

At Inspire we recommend defining your personal purpose with this exercise: simply get a piece of paper, then consider, reflect and write down the eight most important things in your life. A good strategy is to first write down around 20 important things and then to narrow it down to eight. Next give each of those items a score out of 10 based on how much time and attention you feel you're giving to each of them, or how well you feel you're doing. An example could be your family, where you might give yourself 5 out of 10 because you have to work some weekends rather than spending time with them, or your health and fitness, where 8 out of 10 could mean going to the gym five times a week and eating well. Be honest about what is important to you and how well you are doing. This will show you where you are focusing your time and energy, and whether you are neglecting those things that matter. It's extremely important that any entrepreneur who wishes to grow their business and is on their journey stops and reflects regularly: I'd actually recommend that everybody does this exercise every three months.

To take the exercise further you can come up with three ideas for each of those eight areas of your life which could improve your score by one point, then commit to undertaking one of those ideas for all eight areas over the next several months. This will give you some focus and direction to improve your personal wellbeing, and to ensure you are focusing on not just your business, but also your personal purpose and what is truly important to you.

INTRODUCING THE CONCEPT OF ONE

When I talk about increasing your score by one what does that really mean? It means that you are committing to taking one Original, Necessary Evolution to move forward: sticking to your ideas and trusting that change will occur. Throughout the book there will be exercises to help you make a change: try to stick to the concept of ONE for all of these; commit to improving by just one point in an area, so that change remains manageable and occurs gradually and consistently. Every small step can be very important, and can change your life and entrepreneurial journey for the better, setting you on a trajectory towards good times.

ESTABLISHING BUSINESS AMBITION

Now that we've established what is important in your life, we need to consider what the ambition of the business should be, and how it should relate to your personal focus. It's this overriding business ambition that will drive its ambition, essence, spirit and beliefs.

Some people have a very clear idea of what their business's ambition and purpose is, others lack a certain clarity and direction. There's a classic story about a cleaner at NASA who was once asked to describe their job, and replied, 'My job is to put a man on the Moon'. The clarity of purpose within NASA as an organisation at the time is clear.

While we may not all be trying to put a man on the Moon, we must still be clear in our ambition and purpose. So what is yours – what are you trying to achieve? What are your big, scary goals? What is your dream? Find a way to answer these questions and articulate that as the purpose why and ambition for your business. This is not what your business *does*, or how you do that, that is its essence. Rather, it's your overarching ambitions for what you want to achieve.

At Inspire our ambition is to enable ambitious and driven entrepreneurs to succeed. It is a really simple and clear statement that the team and those that engage with us can understand.

The challenge when you do stop to reflect on you ambition is that you need to consider it not with your existing perspective and lens but free from that existing narrative.

Others may also describe that ambition as 'the why' and there are a lot of great resources out there on 'how to find your why', just google it. However, based on my personal experience from Inspire and also from working with many ambitious business owners I'd recommend focusing on a term that all can understand. Ambition has great clarity and is relevant for an entrepreneurial business.

Also remember my personal story; the ambition cannot simply be about the money. It may sound strange coming from an accountant, but my firm belief is that rather than focusing on the money, you should focus on creating a great business that delivers for its customers and has true ambition – only then will sustainable profits be generated.

WHAT ARE ESSENCE, SPIRIT AND BELIEFS?

Now we have determined your personal focus and business ambition, let's explore the terms 'essence', 'spirit' and 'beliefs' and what they mean in depth.

ESSENCE

The essence of your business is how you describe and set out how you are going to achieve your ambition. It will become a really clear statement about what you set out to do.

For Inspire our Essence is 'providing relevant, insightful and innovative business and tax advisory services to our niche market of ambitious and driven entrepreneurs'.

In considering your essence also stop, reflect and think about whether you have truly defined your ambition. If you have then it should be a relatively straight forward exercise to set out how you are going to achieve that ambition. Remember however that you should not be constrained by what you simply do now. This is about what the business needs to do to achieve its future ambition. Approaching it this way will provide the business and the team with focus on not just what you are doing now but also what you need to be doing in the future.

SPIRIT

Every entrepreneurial business has a unique sense of energy to it, and a sense of emotion. Effectively a spirit which defines how people behave and interact, and which separates it from the interchangeable corporates. At Inspire our spirit embodies being caring, being positive, being passionate, while being empathetic. Reflect now on what defines the energy of your business.

Spirit can be a little harder to specify than essence, because it refers to the feeling that people get when dealing with your business or when working there. It's created by ensuring that what is important to you is thoroughly instilled in the culture of the business and hiring people that fit with those principles.

Having begun to consider what your business's spirit and energy does / should look and feel like, it may now be helpful to undertake this very simple exercise to refine your ideas. Sit down and reflect on what it feels like in your business. What the energy is like on a really good day. Really pause and consider this: what are the emotional words that you would write down? (Six is enough).

BELIEFS

Your beliefs should be the guiding principles that you and all of those in your business follow, that you want to see demonstrated day in, day out, be that in the interactions with your customers or the way in which you and the team interact with each other. At Inspire our beliefs are that we are straight-talking, we are determined, we exceed expectations, and we're encouraging and supportive.

As you can see, beliefs are more tangible and more reflective of your ability to articulate the required behaviours in the business.

How should you go about establishing the beliefs within your business? There are two simple exercises to do so.

Firstly, stop, think and reflect on what the key principles that underpin your business are. This will tell you what your beliefs are now. However, it does not set the bar for where you want to be. If you're in the valley of despair it's possible that the guiding principles of your business are currently weak.

To set principles going forward, stop and think about three companies that you admire and three that you dislike. Write down all the company names, and next to those write down why you feel that way. You can then take what you've learned – in the context of your personal purpose, previously established – and apply to it your business, in terms of what to aim for and what to avoid in its guiding principles.

LINKING YOUR ESSENCE, SPIRIT AND BELIEFS

Having defined your essence, spirit and beliefs, we can take this further by thinking carefully about how they practically flow through your business, and coming up with simple statements which show how they are linked to real tasks and departments. For example at Inspire, we realized that our spirit and beliefs in particular interacted with three core areas of our business: our offering, our people and our client relationships. Our statements were:

OUR OFFERING

Inspire provides support and advice to our clients by developing **innovative** and **unique** services and solutions that enable our clients to succeed.

OUR PEOPLE

Our people are a team of **passionate** and **talented** individuals that are committed to **exceeding expectations**.

OUR CLIENT RELATIONSHIPS

Inspire's client relationships are **transparent, supportive, empathetic** and **encouraging** while at the same time we are not afraid, while being **caring**, to be **straight talking** such that we give our clients the right advice at the right time to enable them to succeed.

BELONGING V LOYALTY

I also believe that by clearly defining your ambition, essence, spirit and beliefs you will start to create a sense of belonging in the business. Please consider the distinction between creating within a business a sense of belonging versus a sense of loyalty. Stop and think about it ... Those businesses with a great culture, brand and team have within them a great sense of belonging. A sense of belonging brings with it a true bond, greater belief, and a true affinity for what that organisation is setting out to achieve. Versus a situation where team members remain in the team just because they are loyal.

These statements bring meaning to your ambition, essence, spirit and beliefs and why they are important – for you, for your business and for everybody who interacts with it.

ENGAGING YOUR TEAM

The exercises that I propose above are written such that you can personally consider the ambition, essence, spirit and beliefs of your team. However once you have considered these and come up with an outline then the draft needs to be shared with your team. You need to create buy-in from them and it is essential that they feel they have contributed. In a larger business with an established senior leadership team I would also recommend undertaking these exercises in their entirety with the team to gain the engagement needed.

Once you have finalised the ambition, essence, spirit and beliefs for the business you then need to communicate them in a passionate and appropriate fashion with the entire business and importantly I've found benefit in sharing with key clients and suppliers as well.

REINVENTION, REJUVENATION AND GROWTH

Ambition, spirit and beliefs become most important for your business during periods of reinvention, rejuvenation or growth. These are the periods when you are most susceptible to dilution – when lots of new team members are coming on board. They may well have an excitement to join you and the journey that you're on, but dilution can occur in the way you want business to be conducted, how you want people to interact as a team, how you want people to interact with and deliver to your customers. The recruitment process has to be undertaken by people who fully understand the ambition, essence, spirit and beliefs of your business, ensuring that this is a part of every contact with candidates and a key criteria for selection.

If you truly implement and let your ambition, essence, spirit and beliefs flow through everything in your business, and if they are at the heart of every period of reinvention or rejuvenation you go through, your business is sure to scale and succeed without diluting that initial focus, passion and belief that you had on day one. Remember that original focus, passion and belief when reignited does not just give you the drive to succeed but when communicating in this way your team's focus passion and belief enables the business to succeed.

At Inspire, after realising we were in the valley of despair and stripping the business back, came the period of rejuvenation. I injected my ambition, essence, spirit and beliefs into every aspect of the business, and four years on I continue to do so and see positive results. My team members are appraised in line with my ambition, essence, spirit and beliefs. When I profile and question new employees who are coming on board, they're questioned to see whether they suit and fit my ambition, essence, spirit and beliefs. When I'm taking on new clients, I look at them, their business and the values that can be demonstrated within that business, and whether they too align with my ambition, essence, spirit and beliefs. Because if there is conflict and there is not alignment, that's an early sign that the client journey is not going to be smooth, or the team member is not going to work out: it's a sign that you're not going to build a successful long-term relationship.

Avoid the corporate trap of just believing that ambition, essence, spirit and beliefs are a vision and mission statement to be written down and occasionally referred to. They're not. They're something to live and breathe by. They're something that should be reflected in everyday life within your business. Do this and you will rapidly see the difference.

CHAPTER KEY QUESTIONS
AND EXERCISES

Key questions and exercises that you should consider from this chapter are:

- Undertake the exercise to define your personal purpose and the eight most important things to you.

- What was your greatest insight from undertaking the personal purpose exercise?

- What was your original ambition for the business?

- How do you think that original ambition and focus has evolved?

- Define you current business ambition.

- Define your essence, spirit and beliefs using the exercises.

- How can you link your essence, spirit and beliefs such that they integrate into your business?

- What do you need to do right now to rejuvenate your business and personal energy?

CHAPTER 3

Personal Development

In your journey as an entrepreneur it's easy to put everything you have into the business, working long hours with an unwavering focus. Both your physical and mental health, and that mythical work-life balance are thrown to the wayside in the name of pushing things forward. But, as I'll explore in this chapter, this is a not a productive strategy for the long-term success of your business. Taking time out not only recharges your batteries and keeps you healthy for the long entrepreneurial journey, but also gives you perspective of the bigger picture: on what is important to develop in the business and what to leave behind.

This chapter will also talk about the need for continuous personal development of your skills and also gaining a better understanding of yourself. Having a good mentor can be invaluable. In addition, trusting in your team enough to take time away yourself, allowing them to run things for a while and develop, will also build the strengths of the business as a whole.

Personal development is, unfortunately, often overlooked in the mad dash towards success. But those who take time to do it ultimately end up leading their businesses further and gaining significantly more success than those who choose not to. Jim Rohn put it perfectly when he said: 'Your level of success will rarely exceed your level of personal development, because success is something you attract by the person you become.'

SELF-AWARENESS

The first step when it comes to proactively taking care of your well-being and self-development is to have a very close awareness of your own personal "state". Leading entrepreneurs and successful business owners often seem to be in complete balance with themselves, taking care of their health and achieving their perfect vision for the business, and they do so through acute self-awareness.

This means knowing when you're pushing your body too hard and are on the point of getting sick, when you've been in the office too much and your family are paying the price, and it means knowing the gaps in your skillset and knowledge which have held you back and which need to be filled by working on your development. It also means knowing your personal values and motivations inside out. I've talked about this a lot already in Chapters 1 and 2, but this knowledge is vital for self-development because it means you will have a clear picture of how you want your business to evolve, and as a result will know how you need to evolve personally to achieve your ambition. Compare this to the entrepreneur with no self-awareness whatsoever, who ploughs forwards blindly and inevitably stumbles into a self-destruct button, ending up in the valley of despair.

It can be useful to ask yourself the following questions. Do this often and really focus on giving an honest answer to each. You can then take action accordingly.

- What sacrifices am I making right now in terms of health or relationships, and are they truly worth it? Could I make some adjustments to better balance my life?

- What are my distractions? What am I giving my focus to which is not helping my long-term goal? Which of these are positive (e.g. family, hobbies, fitness) and which are negative? (e.g. working hard on a project which is not a core part of the business or which is not contributing to the ambition of the business).

- What does success look like to me personally? What would good times feel like? Not what would be good for the business, but what is important to me? What would personal good times feel like?

- Are the behaviours demonstrated in the business aligned to my personal values?

Taking some regular time out to think about these simple questions will keep you focused on your path, and will ensure you maintain a strong sense of self-awareness.

WHAT YOU WANT TO BE, DO AND HAVE

A proven coaching technique that I believe works really well is to decide what you want to be, do and have. It is very important to understand this for your own personal development. So what does this actually mean? 'Be' is about who you are, what you mean to other people, your character, your values, your ambition: fundamentally it is what you want to be remembered for. 'Do' is what you want to achieve and experience: how do you really want to spend your time and your life? And finally 'have': this means the things and possessions that are of value to you; what are the things in life that you enjoy, such as health, wealth and security.

The following is a simple example of the Be, Do, Have model:

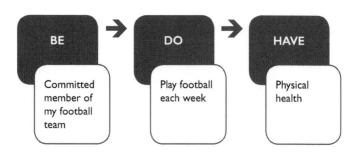

The order 'have, do, be' suggests a victim entrepreneur mindset, with the thinking pattern, 'If only I had more time / money etc. I would be able to do great things and be great'.

The second category is the entrepreneurial worker, where the order is 'do, have, be'. Their thinking pattern is, 'If I do all these things, I will have what I want and prove who I am'.

The final category is the entrepreneurial winner, where the order is 'be, do, have'. They think, 'If I behave according to my ambition and values, I will be able to do and have what I want, and achieve my goals in life'.

Really consider which of these you are, and be honest with yourself if you need to work on a mindset shift. The truth is that many of us, including me, strive to be entrepreneurial winners but are in fact experts at being entrepreneurial workers.

Spend some time writing down what you really want in these three areas. To interpret what you've found, rank the categories 'be', 'do' and 'have' in order of importance.

WELL-BEING

For every single entrepreneur out there, the stresses and strains of running a business are guaranteed to take some kind of toll, whether mental, physical or both. Self-awareness allows you to recognise this. But having taken stock of how you're doing, it's important to then actually take action to maintain or improve your well-being. Whatever you do, don't ignore the problem. Make changes where you can, and seek external professional help if you think it's necessary. Be really honest with yourself here: you can't run a business if your body and mind are broken.

I have seen it happen so many times; where entrepreneurs have stopped exercising, eat worse food, drink more alcohol and sleep very little. These things gradually creep up on them as they become busier and busier. But to perform at a high level mentally the body has to be taken care of: being fit and healthy means you still have energy at the end of the day rather than feeling lethargic, and it means being able to think clearly rather than having a mind fogged by tiredness and a false and short-lived sugar or caffeine high.

The key question with well-being is: is what I'm doing sustainable? We can all push the boundaries to achieve certain goals, but this is only possible for so long before things begin to deteriorate, whether that be neglecting our personal lives, our health, or working without taking a break for hours and hours at a time. If you are pushing your boundaries, take note that at some point you will have to scale back and find a balance, else you will ultimately burnout and self-destruct. For your business to succeed you need to find a sustainable path which takes into account all aspects of well-being, so that you can lead effectively.

So stop and ask yourself the question, am I in a sustainable position?

If you are in a position that doesn't feel sustainable, gradually you will have to make more and more compromises with worse and worse results. Whatever activity you are doing you will not be 100 % present because there are too many things taxing your mind. Really be honest with yourself, prioritise what needs to be cut back, and do it. Every now and again you will be able to push the boundaries as needed, but will always return to that state of sustainable balance. There's no magic wand for getting to this state – everyone's solution is different and depends on what is truly important to them. Every solution will mean some kind of sacrifice, but it's a necessary one for the long-term well-being of you and your business.

THE WORK LIFE BALANCE MYTH AND POWER OF BEING PRESENT

It may sound controversial, but as entrepreneurs there's no such thing as a 'work/life' balance. We don't work 9-5 and spend every weekend with our loved ones or doing the other things we love to do in life. We're entrepreneurs 24/7. But this doesn't mean we should abandon our family, friends and other interests. It means that when we do spend time with the people we love and are doing the other things we love in life we should be 100% present. That means NOT secretly thinking about the to-do list or what is happening in the business! We also have freedom from not working 9-5, which is a real positive and therefore make use of this freedom and ensure by being 100% present you get the opportunity to enjoy those unique special moments in time that can be captured.

POWER OF
ACCOUNTABILITY PARTNERS

Another point on well-being is around the issue of loneliness as a business leader – of being unable to share stories of trials and tribulations with people who really 'get it' and understand. Although friends and family can be sympathetic, it's difficult for them to comprehend the strain you're under without having experienced it themselves. As such, it can be very helpful to become part of an entrepreneurial peer group. Here you'll have like-minded individuals in the room who have had similar experiences and will more fully understand your stories. Having people like this to share the experience of your journey with and gain new ideas from can be really important.

If there is not a peer group for you then instead consider finding your own accountability partner; someone experiencing the same journey as you that you can relate to. Effectively an accountability partner is someone to meet up with regularly either in a formal or informal environment and who you can share your ambitions, issues, challenges, and what is working and not working with, as well as someone to bounce ideas off. Spend, say, half an hour doing this, but more importantly set commitments to each other on actions, timescales and deadlines so you can keep one another on track and accountable. This is becoming an invaluable process to me.

HABITS

There is a myth that creating a new habit can take just 21 days, but research has shown that in fact it takes an average of 66 days, and up to 254 days.

However, the length of time it takes is not the important factor here. What is important is how habits, and changing habits, can have a huge impact on your personal development and ability to succeed, as well as on the business and your team. Creating new habits can support your goals and objectives, both personally and within the business.

A habit is the result of the continual pursuit of this clear goal, taking one step at a time in the right direction. And by its very nature, once in place a habit requires little conscious effort to maintain. That means if you set up many good habits your life will be steered in the right direction on autopilot. This is very thought-provoking if you stop and reflect on it.

So how do you go about setting up a good habit or eradicating a bad one? My experience shows that for a habit to change there always has to be a goal or desire, a vision for the future, followed by the necessary behaviour to make that change, and finally you must know what the reward is for doing so.

There are three typical stages in the change process: the first is the honeymoon period, just after we have set our new goals and objectives and expressed a desire to create new habits. A typical example of this period is January 1st with our new year's resolutions. At this point we feel inspired and are easily motivated.

The second stage is the fight period: this is a couple of weeks in when we realise that our goals are not easily achievable, that they are going to take work. It's January 14th and many resolutions are about to be abandoned. It's also here that limiting beliefs begin to kick in (more on this in the next section). When in this stage it's essential that we realise that's where we are, and work hard to challenge and change our habits. We need to understand it, and we need to connect deeply with the emotions associated with the guaranteed positive outcome that will result from changing our habit. Look to the future, and really try to feel the pain of having the same life that you have now, compared to the pleasure of having the life you want as a result of new habits.

Finally we have the second nature stage. This comes once the habit has been created, whether it took 21, 66 or 254 days. The new behaviour has begun to feel habitual, and no longer requires much conscious effort to accomplish. However, this period can still be deemed dangerous: there will always be naysayers, disruptions such as holidays, or the seduction of a seemingly easy route to success. All these can knock you out of your good habits, so be mindful and pay attention. Be strong in the knowledge of what you want to achieve and how – and trust that your good habits are the way to get there.

I challenge you as an individual to try to form one new habit per quarter. Identify a habit that would be key in helping you get one step closer towards a long-term goal, and run with it. If you think about it, doing just this, gaining one useful new habit a quarter, will mean that you are four steps further along your entrepreneurial journey by the end of the year.

So stop and reflect right now. Write down a habit that you want to establish for this quarter, and commit to working through the fight phase until it is second nature.

LIMITING BELIEFS

Limiting beliefs exert a huge amount of control and influence over all aspects of our lives, be that personal or business. A key point here is that everyone has limiting beliefs, but those who truly succeed manage to uncover and recognise them. This can be a really difficult process, but if you can overcome your limiting beliefs, your chances of ultimate success will be exponentially greater.

So why are they difficult to uncover and overcome? It's because many of us see our limiting beliefs as cold hard facts, rather than as something that could be changed. Subconsciously we are programmed to ignore or fight any evidence which contradicts our beliefs, and find and notice any evidence which supports them. Most of us will have both helpful and limiting beliefs which make up our reality, and our goal should always be to try to replace disempowering beliefs with empowering beliefs, so that our belief system takes us in a positive direction.

How, then, do we uncover some of these limiting beliefs? Simply take some time to answer the following questions honestly:

- What rules have you set yourself that limit you?

- What pessimistic thoughts do you have?

- What are your recurring narratives that hold you back?

- What values might be holding you back?

- Are there any cultural or stereotypical barriers holding you back?

- What evidence exists to disprove any of the above?

- What evidence exists to support more positive beliefs?

These questions can be difficult to answer, because you really have to face yourself and be totally rational; that is why limiting beliefs can be so difficult to overcome. Trying to do so alone can be even more difficult, but these questions will point you in the right direction. To make things easier a strong personal mentor or coach will often be able to help you greatly with this, as long as they are non-judgemental and trustworthy, and as long as you are open, honest and share your true feelings with them about what might be holding you back.

This is what I personally did: I found a life coach and worked with them to overcome some of my own limiting beliefs that stemmed from the fact I left school early and hadn't gone to university. I felt inadequate in the company of those in business who were highly educated, who perhaps came from a better background than myself. Looking back on it, and considering all that I'd achieved by that point, these were crazy thoughts stemming from a faulty belief system, and they certainly held me back. But with my coach's help I was able to overcome these beliefs, grow as an individual and continue to succeed.

As an individual you need to believe in your own greatness, be grateful and recognise who you are and what you've achieved. A positive mindset is essential for this. Only then will you be able to move past your limiting beliefs to reach your full potential: I encourage you to stop and reflect now on how you might do this.

GAINING PERSPECTIVE

You often hear about successful entrepreneurs taking time away from their business, and are perhaps wondering how they could ever do this – how could their business continue to grow? The truth is that the occasional break is not only necessary for well-being (try working for six months straight without a break, it's a disaster waiting to happen), but can also give you the distance needed to be able to gain real perspective. To rise above the trees to see the forest.

Many of us can get stuck in a mode where we're putting in lots of effort and it feels like we're getting a lot done, but in actual fact we're achieving absolutely nothing. This could be because our brains are fried from overwork, or it could be because we've lost perspective on what's important and we're focusing our efforts on worthless areas.

These breaks from work are often the times when big moments of realisation happen. And so recognising that the most successful entrepreneurs take these breaks, and following their lead, could be a big help for you and your business. When you're going at 100 miles per hour, let's face it, there's no real planning going on. You're just continuing as fast as possible down the path you originally followed with no strategic thinking. But is that still the correct path, and are you indeed still on it? Slowing down and getting some distance is the only way to be sure.

As kids we were told that if we work hard we'll succeed. That if we knuckle down and put in the hours we'll do well. Nobody told us the real truth: that working smart, planning your time carefully, and checking in regularly that what you're doing is correct, is the best path to success. For many people this is an ingrained belief system from school that has to be consciously challenged and changed as an adult.

PERCEPTION OF VALUE

Credit to the illustration that follows and its simple thought-provoking nature goes to Neil Crespin, founder and creative director of MCM Creative Group, who, when he presented it at an Inspire conference, blew the audience away. When I first saw it I was taken aback by its simplicity. But it will lead you to some important conclusions, and begin to put into perspective the value that you assign to various things in your life, whether that's possessions, relationships, or goals achieved.

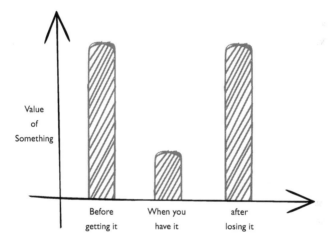

Many of us will know the desire, the need and the feeling of hunger when we set our sights on achieving something, or adding something to our life: it will have a really high perceived value. But when we actually have that thing, do we continue to value it?

Do we really consider its worth and appreciate it once it's ours? Do we take for granted our friends, family and relationships?

For those of us who have lost that hard-won desired object, or that relationship, or have experienced the loss of a family member or friend, we know the value of something after it has gone. And if you're honest with yourself and reflect, I'm sure you'll agree that the value of something lost seems so much greater afterwards than when you had it. Indeed, its perceived value is probably similar to before you got it, when it was still something to achieve.

Take a moment to stop and think about this very simple illustration, and about the things you currently have in your life – both the tangible and intangible. Try to be as honest as possible. How are you really valuing them? And how would it feel if you lost them?

WARREN'S STORY: COMPROMISE

Being driven and ambitious, I've always struggled with the conflict between work and family life. Early on in the Inspire story, about seven months in, we had gained our first really significant transaction advising a client on how to undertake buying a fairly significant technology business. I'd thrown myself heart and soul into this transaction, as at that time there were only three of us in the business.

All of a sudden news came that my little daughter Alex was about to be born. I rushed to the hospital, and soon after we brought home our new baby girl. But then within an hour of arriving back home I was on a conference call trying to make this deal happen. I shut myself away for the first few weeks of my daughter's life, and it's something that I look back on with a great deal of regret – I can hardly even believe that I did it. Those weeks can never be brought back, and I have very few memories from them other than of the pressures of the client deal.

In hindsight, of course, I realise that my priorities were not in order, that my balance was completely off-kilter. And it's a lesson that I've had to learn the hard way by missing some of the most special moments a father can have. As entrepreneurs, although we often have to make sacrifices and compromises to get the job done, we should be very careful about what compromises we are making. I made the compromise of missing my daughter's first few weeks in order to make a deal: believe me, if you ever make a compromise like that, it will come back to haunt you for a very long time.

It hit me hard not long after the deal was complete, and the impact could have quite easily caused me to self-destruct and the business to fail. Luckily I got my head straight by following the principles and doing the exercises that you find in this book, putting everything in my life and business in perspective and coming up with new ways to move forward. Since then, every decision I have made has been with a great deal of self-awareness and a careful measuring of my priorities and well-being. Destroying your personal life by overworking will do absolutely nothing good for the business; it will almost inevitably lead you to the valley of despair. But if you do find yourself there, I strongly believe that you can climb out as a better and stronger entrepreneur by following the principles and exercises provided.

SELF-DEVELOPMENT

As entrepreneurs we all hope and expect that our businesses will grow, evolve and scale. However, for this to happen we as business leaders must also develop and evolve. There is a fairly common problem among entrepreneurs where this simply doesn't happen; the entrepreneur achieves some success with the skills and abilities they already have – which comprise the innate entrepreneurial flair that is usually required for early success – but then hit a brick wall because they believe these initial skills and abilities are enough.

Consider a football player, who has worked hard their whole life to turn professional; do they stop training and working hard on their abilities after they go pro? Of course not. And neither should entrepreneurs. Larger businesses have different requirements from their leader than startups – continuous self-development is the only way to keep adapting to these changing needs so that the business can continue to grow, scale and evolve.

Personal development can also mean things not directly related to work, but which still affect it. For example, learning about nutrition and fitness will help your well-being and therefore effectiveness at work. And taking time to establish your personal values could clarify for you what you truly care about (see Chapter 2 for more on finding out what is truly important to you).

Strong self-awareness here means that you know exactly what you are lacking, and therefore what you need to work on.

However, self-development is also one of the most important areas for you to get help and guidance from other people, whether that be a mentor, a personal trainer, a life coach, a nutritionist, etc. Often as entrepreneurs we are so busy and there is so much neglect in our lives that it can be incredibly helpful to have people to hold us to account on our personal development goals.

Having this steady focus on personal development will help you gain clarity and focus, and will always help to bring you back to the fundamental building blocks: focus, passion and belief in your business. Without development you will find that you and your business will stagnate and slide into the valley of despair.

So the critical question is what are your own self development needs?

THE POWER OF A MENTOR

Following on from this, I would highly recommend that every business leader get a good mentor. 'We all need a Yoda', so to speak. Most entrepreneurs are focused, determined, strong characters, and so often the people around them won't tell them the hard truths, the things they don't want to hear. Being surrounded by 'yes men', however well-intentioned (or perhaps because they're scared of losing their jobs), can become very dangerous if the entrepreneur thinks that everything is going swimmingly when in fact it's falling apart.

Having one or two people to talk to who you respect, who will challenge your ideas and ask the difficult questions, can be invaluable on both a personal and business level. It can raise your self-awareness, provide important guidance and someone to confide in when your closest friends may not understand.

The important thing with a mentor is to find the right person for you. Don't just be happy with the first person who you come across in your industry. Keep your eyes wide open, talk to people, make lots of connections, and ask someone who you think could really help you and tell you the truth. It doesn't have to be somebody who already knows you – it could be someone that's prominent in your industry, who's already been on a journey like yours – or it could be a close personal friend. The key is to keep your eyes and mind open, otherwise you'll never find the right mentor.

Also, don't be afraid to ask. Be brave and pick up the phone. This person may be hugely successful, sitting on the board of a multimillion pound company, but they may well still want to be a mentor. And of course, if you don't ask, you are guaranteed to not get anything!

You might wonder why someone like this would want to mentor someone who hasn't yet made much of an impact in the industry. The fact is that they may be coming to the end of their career and want to give something back, or it could be really rewarding for them to help someone with ambition, drive and who is just starting out on their journey. They might even learn something themselves from the situations you talk to them about. And for all these reasons, as you progress further on your journey, you should consider being a mentor as well. Keep your eyes open not only for those who can help you, but those who you could help.

A quick note on paid mentorship programmes organised by specific companies. Although there are some good ones out there, generally speaking I would advise against going for these. This is because you want your mentor to be doing it out of passion and a love for the industry, or because they believe in you – not just because they're getting paid by a third party. Would such a mentor really ask you the difficult questions if that meant risking getting fired as a mentor with no more money? In addition, you will probably have more respect for and a better relationship with a mentor that you find yourself, rather than one that you were simply assigned from a pool.

So take the first steps now to find your Yoda. Pick up that pen and write down three people you could approach to help mentor you and then then make the approach to each in your order of preference.

SELF-DEVELOPMENT, WELL-BEING AND YOUR TEAM

Self-development is not solely about you as the entrepreneur – it is also an issue that concerns, affects and shapes your team.

BETTER SELF-DEVELOPMENT MEANS BETTER PEOPLE

First of all, an entrepreneur who is constantly looking to better themselves in relevant ways for the sake of the business will attract higher-quality people to the team. People who are also interested in bettering themselves, and as a result bettering the business. It may not be obvious that this is going on, but it seems to be a universal rule that positive and successful people attract other positive and successful people. And an entrepreneur who has a refreshed sense of focus, drive and purpose thanks to self-development will recognise this in others too.

MAKING SURE YOUR TEAM HAS GOOD WELL-BEING AND SELF-DEVELOPMENT

I mentioned earlier in the chapter the importance of self-awareness for personal well-being and development. Alongside this should be a careful awareness of how your team is doing and what they need, as well as what their gaps in skills / knowledge are and how best to go about filling them. As the entrepreneur, it goes without saying, you should be caring, supportive and offer guidance at the appropriate time. But equally it's up to you to try to instil a culture in the company where people look out for these things themselves and take action, so that over time you can rest assured that the team will take care of itself.

By becoming a more self-aware leader you ensure that you don't drive your team too hard, that they are motivated to keep developing and improving in their careers, and that you generally have a strong, healthy team. And when the business leader has a well-balanced life and comes into the office every day with energy, focus and passion, the positive effect in the office will be palpable: this is leading by example.

LEADERSHIP SKILLS

While leading by example is great, there is a great deal more to good leadership than this, and while there are some entrepreneurs out there who are naturally good at leadership, most of us are not. For your team and your business to truly grow, scale and thrive, you need to be a great leader. Ensure that as part of your self-development you learn more about how to lead. Read books, go on leadership courses, talk to your mentors, get coaching – there is no one-size-fits-all approach to this, but ensure that you do it.

I would summarise leadership by stating that if you want to scale then being an entrepreneur is not enough, you need to become an incredible leader.

COMBINING DELEGATION WITH PLAYING TO YOUR STRENGTHS AND UNIQUE ABILITIES

At some point as the business develops you need to ensure that you find a way to play to your own strengths and unique abilities as an entrepreneur. It is the only real way that the business can evolve. The concept of playing to strengths and unique abilities is something that you should also apply to everyone in your team. When I realised the importance of this simple concept and I started to implement it within the business it was transformational.

However in order to play to your own strengths and unique abilities then it is inevitable that you are going to have to delegate and 'let go'. This has been one of my own personal challenges that I have had to overcome and it has been one of my biggest lessons. For many years I strived to form a leadership team such that I could delegate and let go but failed on each and every occasion. What I finally learnt was that I had not been emotionally ready to give up the operational reigns, whatever my voice was saying. When I was, it was simple. As a result I also learnt that truly letting go means committing to the decision on every level – dedicating yourself to it, and carrying it out with the same passion and determination you gave to starting the business in the first place.

What's really wonderful is that in letting go I have actually reinvigorated my passion for the business and found my entrepreneurial spirit again. This will happen for you as well once you have a platform where your business is being nurtured, protected and developed such that you can make a greater contribution as a result.

TRUSTING YOUR TEAM

Earlier in this chapter I recommended taking fairly regular time away from the business in order to rest and gain perspective. But there is another great reason for doing this: it develops your team's skills at handling the business when you are not there, and also makes them feel that they are trusted.

It really can be amazing what happens in your business when you're away. People take responsibility and step up, and grow as individuals. It shows you that you don't always have to be the superhero who does everything themselves – you can trust your team. Of course, this requires careful planning and delegation before you leave so that people feel confident to do what needs to be done, but properly executed it will help your business to grow from strength to strength as leadership qualities are developed in the team. It can be difficult for this to happen if you are always around.

CONCLUSION

Hopefully this chapter has given you some insight into how best to look after and develop yourself, and how as a result this will affect your team and the business as a whole for the better. The key is to start with true self-awareness: don't run or hide from the truth, look at yourself as objectively as you can and figure out how best to fix or improve what you see, so that you have a positive and sustainable course ahead.

Remember also the importance of holistic success. What I mean by this is to remember that success means so much more than professional triumphs. Over recent years I have pushed myself massively as an individual, but I have also practiced self-nurturing. I've developed a fitness regime, I've changed my diet, I've improved my sleep, and I've recognised my limits. But most importantly, I have tried to be kinder to myself. Now, I'm not saying that I am succeeding on all those fronts, far from it at times. But I am doing what I would ask you to do: I am giving myself the time and attention I deserve and am feeling healthier and happier because of it.

And remember with a positive mindset you can control your own life and importantly create the life you want to live! Do this and you'll reap the rewards on so many levels.

CHAPTER KEY QUESTIONS
AND EXERCISES

Key questions and exercises that you should consider from this chapter are:

- Undertake the exercise to consider the key questions relating to self-awareness and draw an overall conclusion on your own self-awareness and where focus is required.

- Undertake the exercise to establish what you want to be, do and have.

- Are you in a sustainable position?

- Join a peer group or find an accountability partner.

- Commit to changing at least one habit in the next quarter.

- Respond to the key questions on limiting beliefs and conclude what are your limiting beliefs?

- How are you going to eradicate your limiting beliefs?

- What are your own self development needs?

- Who's your Yoda?

- How can you improve your own leadership skills?

CHAPTER 4

Business Fundamentals

Up until this point in the book I have focused mainly on the values and mindsets that help to build a successful business, and help it transition and scale while keeping its energy and passion intact. This chapter explores these ideas from a more practical perspective. I'll be taking a look at the business fundamentals which go hand in hand with your ambition, essence, spirit and beliefs and which will ensure continued success.

The key focus of this chapter is on building, training and retaining the best possible team. Having the right people is absolutely fundamental to achieving your vision for the business, being client-centric, and delivering client delight, and there are many pitfalls in this area. I will also cover principles for leadership, the business model, planning, including how to be strategic in an entrepreneurial business and how to develop effective KPIs, and some marketing basics.

There are, of course, other important areas of any business which entrepreneurs must be aware of and focus on, but there are so many other books out there which cover other fundamentals in great detail that I would recommend you go to those resources if you would like more information. This book will cover the aspects most closely linked to the ambition, essence, spirit and beliefs of a business.

KEY PRINCIPLES AND NOT A COOKIE CUTTER MODEL

When it comes to designing a business model, there are many resources available which give set-in-stone, copy-and-paste structures for running a business. But entrepreneurial organisations by their very nature are full of quirks and have unique qualities which set them apart, this is what makes them awesome. Trying to fit these businesses into a pre-set model is as effective as fitting a square peg into a round hole; it will turn an entrepreneurial business into a faceless corporate and mean they lose the features which set them apart in the first place.

There are a myriad of different methodologies, processes, elements and strategies that you can build and evolve in a dynamic entrepreneurial business, but all of them adhere to certain core principles. By focusing on these principles, entrepreneurs can adapt and be creative with their strategies, moulding them to suit their company's unique needs, while still creating a business model that performs. I learned the hard way at Inspire that 'winging it' doesn't work: you can't succeed without systems, processes and a model. But equally your imaginative and entrepreneurial spirit needs to be able to shine through, not be stifled by a model that doesn't fit.

For entrepreneurs that are in the valley of despair, it's often the case that the wheels have begun to spin too fast on their business and they've lost focus on what is really important. Things can feel out of control and they will seem to meet the same challenges wherever they turn, becoming increasingly frustrated that the changes and evolution they wish to see are failing to manifest. As this happens it's easy to lose sight of why they began the business in the first place: the personal values and goals that always exist at the start of the journey. For these entrepreneurs, the principles in this chapter can act as a guiding light to steer the business back to its original focus. By coming back to the core of why the entrepreneur began their startup, by simplifying their model and by carefully selecting their team and customer base, they can begin to gain a better understanding of their business and find a way to drive things forward with much more clarity.

BUSINESS PLANNING

Consider this question: from your own experience, does your business's growth come from a predetermined business strategy, or does it come from seizing unexpected opportunities? Not surprisingly, most entrepreneurs that I have worked with respond to that question by saying that seizing opportunity has played a huge part in their success. However, my conclusion from many years of experience is that successful businesses and entrepreneurs do both.

This leads us to the dreaded subject of business planning. In my time advising entrepreneurs and ambitious business owners I have seen so much entrepreneurial spirit and initiative quashed and killed as a business grows, often via a 'consultant' coming in and insisting that growth will be achieved by putting together a detailed business plan. This process ends up with a big, daunting plan that took months and months to produce and is already out of date by the time it is finalised. In the entrepreneurial world it inevitably ends up languishing in a desk drawer never to see the light of day.

In my opinion a detailed formal plan may work in the corporate environment, but is not appropriate for the entrepreneurial world. In fact it can do significant damage to an entrepreneurial business that is used to being quick and nimble on its feet, and seeks opportunity. This doesn't mean that annual objectives should not be set, or that a plan and direction should not be in place: simply that it's best to keep it simple and straightforward.

Let me tell you how I approach this at Inspire. Before the start of each new financial year I sit down and reflect on the journey over the previous 12 months, consider what good times might look like for us now, and determine what needs to be done over the next 12 and 24 months to achieve it. I set the direction, and communicate this to the directors and senior leadership team. After getting their input, I modify the plan as needed and share it with the entire team in small briefing sessions. There's no huge state of the nation: I like to share with small groups at a time so they feel they can give their feedback and input as well.

Focus in our world is on the non-financial objectives. This might sound strange for an accountant to say, but by focusing on these key goals for the business, the financials will fall into place. The plan we then follow, and measure our progress against by putting in key performance indicators (KPIs), is a simple 12-page presentation.

That said, we do have a longer strategic plan, which was built by setting out what we wanted to achieve over a three-year period.

Once this plan was agreed, each member of the senior team presented on how they were going to achieve a certain aspect of our long-term goals, and how they would measure this on a monthly basis.

When it comes to business planning, my advice is to do it, but keep it simple and communicate it well. Ensure everyone knows how they fit into the plan and what they are responsible for, and that the necessary measurables are in place to track progress. The structure of this simple business planning methodology is shown in the diagram on the opposte page.

The 9 Step Plan to Success

7 Core Areas

- Technology
- Finance
- Operations
- Leadership/Culture
- People/Team
- Product/Service/Innovation
- Sales/Marketing

1 Understand where your business truly is right now.

2 Identify and focus on the non financial objectives first then build the financial plan.

3 Detail the achievements needed in the 7 core areas that are required to deliver your goal.

4 Share with Senior team and get their input—adjust where needed.

5 Senior team sets the operational objectives and actions in line with the core goals.

6 Review the objectives and ensure they can be simply understood, agree by who and by when.

7 Communicate to the wider organisation.

8 Get their input and secure buy-in.

9 Regularly report against measurables and communicate performance across the business.

BUILDING YOUR TEAM

At the centre of any good business model is the right team. Too many entrepreneurs try to do everything themselves, to such an extent that the business would totally fail without them. However real value is built by surrounding yourself with the right people and allowing them to take some of the load; a good team is probably the most important contributing factor to success.

It's also important that we use the word 'team' here, rather than 'staff' or 'employees' – these corporate labels to some extent dehumanise the people who work in your business. The worst thing you can do is to treat them as employee numbers in a spreadsheet. Instead think of them like a professional high-performing sports team. You pick your players, you motivate them, and you get them working together cohesively for great results. This is often how entrepreneurial businesses get their edge over the larger competition: they have the power to individually infuse each member of the team with passion and motivation so that they perform at their highest possible level and deliver client delight.

When talking about team it's also important to remember that this includes everyone who has direct contact with you and who contributes to the business and the energy in the business. This not only includes people who are directly employed, but also contractors, consultants and advisors. When communicating and motivating the team, it's important to be consistent across all the different stakeholders in the business – by considering outside contractors as part of your team and treating them and key suppliers as such they will be infused with that same passion as those directly employed.

PUTTING THE SPOTLIGHT ON THE TEAM

The first step to building a great team is to ensure that a spotlight is always pointed at this area. One of your primary focuses in your business should always be having the right people, doing the right things, in the right way. This spotlight will also help with retention – which I'll talk about later in the chapter – because once you have the right people, the spotlight will ensure that they stay motivated, encouraged, are constantly developing and are rewarded properly.

The spotlight will first reveal who you already have in your team: what are their strengths and weaknesses, what motivates them? This gives you a snapshot of the skills, characters and attributes that are currently missing from the team and allows you to build a recruitment plan.

Another part of the spotlight should be on the future of the team and the business. When building your recruitment plan it can be very tempting to simply fill seats as quickly as possible in the roles which you think you need right now. But this is crisis mode thinking, not strategic thinking. You have to look at your growth path and consider what you might need in three to five years' time. If you then recruit with both the present and future needs of the business in mind, you'll have set yourself up well with a great team for the future as the business evolves.

This may even mean recruiting slightly more people than you need right now to allow room for growth. As a new business with ambition the only way to really grow is if you have the capacity to take on new ideas and new challenges, as well as people to develop the new products and services. Also, to provide great customer service and client delight you really do need that extra capacity. It's important not to think of this as 'slack' but rather capacity that you have exciting plans to use.

So stop and ask yourself the question, what is your perfect future team?

THE ENTREPRENEUR AND THE TEAM

As an entrepreneur who most likely started out alone or with a very small team, it can be difficult to get out of the mode where you like feel you need to do everything yourself. But when you begin to build your team, it's important to know your own strengths and weaknesses, and hire people who are strong where you are weak.

Not only does this mean that you have a better team overall, with everyone playing to their strengths; it also means that you are freed up to take on more of a leadership role, and can avoid getting bogged down in tasks that you simply don't want to do. If running the business begins to feel like a corporate job, you should realise that you are doing the wrong tasks and are heading for the valley of despair, and that it's time to hire the right people and delegate to them.

There are many different kinds of people out there: as an entrepreneur you are probably more creative, flitting between new ideas and exciting possibilities; but for a business to thrive you need balance; for example, people who are good at building systems and efficiency. It takes a broad range of personality types to create a balanced team. It's one of the great things about the world we live in, that whatever task you might hate there will be somebody out there who loves it; find that person and hire them!

A good way to think about it is that the team are there to protect and support the entrepreneur's ability to be entrepreneurial: to be creative, to be high energy, to bring new ideas to the table and to keep their focus tightly on the original values and aspirations of the startup. These are the reasons the entrepreneur began their business, and these are the reasons that they will want to continue putting all their energy into it. Building a strong senior team is especially important to prevent disengagement, lack of motivation, and the gradual erosion of their joy in the business. They can take on some of the leader's day-to-day responsibilities so that they are free to do what they're best at, rather than getting bogged down by all sorts of daily tasks they have no interest in.

I'll look in more detail at what leadership should involve and how to go about it later in the chapter.

RECRUITMENT

Once you have analysed your team and yourself, found where the gaps are and considered capacity for the future, it's time to actually begin hiring. However, finding quality talent is often one of the greatest challenges for young businesses. Unemployment in most western countries is low, and will most likely remain that way for the foreseeable future, so competition is fierce. Having a robust process is a must. In this book I'll cover some of the key aspects of recruitment but do feel free to read any of the many resources out there devoted to the topic.

For entrepreneurial businesses it's essential to leverage your uniqueness in the recruitment process and differentiate yourself from the larger corporate companies to attract people. You are almost never going to be able to compete on salary alone, so it's best to focus on where you add value in other areas. We're all very familiar with the idea of building a brand to be customer-facing to attract new clients, but your brand should also be attractive to talent. Are you seen as a great place to work? Or only as a great service / product provider? There can be many advantages to working at an entrepreneurial business: they tend to be more fun, more challenging, more diverse, more accepting of flexible working, among other things. But the question is, even if all this is true of your business, does anybody know about it? You have to put it out there as an integral part of your employee brand and infuse it into the recruitment process.

As you grow you need to put as much time and effort into developing your employer brand as you do your core brand.

Now that you are looking like an attractive proposition to candidates, you can move onto your gap analysis and see what skills and attributes are required. But don't focus on these at the expense of your ambition, essence, spirit and beliefs during the recruitment process: these are what differentiate your business and make it special. You want people in your team who not only have the right skills, but who also have the right personality and will contribute positively to the energy of the business. Try to ensure that an applicant's spirit and beliefs align with yours; that way when the role grows they will be likely to grow with it.

This brings us onto a second important point. Ensure that you know exactly what the role entails, and what you want it to entail in the future. What kind of person would be good for the role now, and also as it evolves? This is more than just knowing the job specification – although it's really important to have a tight, accurate spec – it's about knowing why that role is needed in the business, and how it fits into the overall business plan going forward. Even if you're recruiting into a well-established team for a role that already exists, and you believe you know exactly what is needed, take the time to have a conversation with someone who you value in the business who is already performing that role. Ask them what the key parts of their job are. Understand what their key characteristics are then incorporate that into the role specification. Be open to this approach and you may be surprised by what you learn.

Be proactive with recruitment

In the current climate of low unemployment, it's very important to think innovatively about where to find good people. While recruitment agencies can be useful partners, this is where the majority of businesses are hunting for talent, and competing directly with others for the same handful of candidates can be difficult. The key is to be proactive, to go out there and find the passive candidates who aren't actively looking for a new job right now.

This could include people who are fairly satisfied with their job but have had thoughts of looking for something new and would be interested in a change, or those who love their work and have no thought whatsoever of leaving their current company. These pools will contain a lot of talent, talent which other companies are probably not targeting. Attracting them away from their current positions can be tricky, however. This is where having a strong and appealing employer brand comes in: you need to give people who are not currently looking for a job a reason to take a look at you.

Technology these days is fantastic for this process: social media allows you to build an easily accessible brand, to get in touch with candidates directly, and to talk to clients who also use competitors to find out which team members they rate in the market. All of this can help you decide who to target for recruitment. Think outside the box and you will attract some great talent into your team.

Mistakes to avoid in the interview process

Part of your employer brand includes how you come across in the interview process, and in my experience this can be where a lot of people fall down. In entrepreneurial businesses in particular, there is often no system in place and interviewers rely on their gut feeling and first impression more than anything else. But this can really backfire: with either a strong or weak first impression the interviewer may not delve deeper and ask challenging questions, or give the candidate more time to show their qualities, because they've already made up their mind. In a candidate-short market you shouldn't write anyone off based on a gut feeling; and equally you shouldn't hire anyone into your business without doing your due diligence and making sure they are as good as the first impression.

To avoid this you must take a disciplined approach with a structured process and set questions that you ask everyone. If you use a two-stage interview process there should be two different interviewers asking different set questions. This creates a level playing field, allows you to find hidden gems who may not shine at first, and avoids hiring the shiny 'fool's gold' candidate who actually would not do well in the role.

In terms of what questions to ask, I strongly believe that you must interview for attitude and aptitude. Technical ability can be trained. Attitude and aptitude can't. A candidate may not have the exact experience required, but if they've shown that they are intelligent and have learnt new skills quickly in the past then you will be able to train them relatively easily. On the other hand a candidate with the exact experience you need but whose personal values do not align with your ambition, essence, spirit and beliefs will quickly pick up the work, and will most likely just as quickly either disrupt the team dynamic or leave. An attitude that doesn't fit can be very difficult to change, and can have serious negative consequences in the business.

Once you have completed your interviews, you should try to decide relatively quickly who to offer the role to, and once this decision has been made you should act immediately. At this point, the interviewer and interviewee roles become somewhat reversed. This comes back to the fact that we are in a candidate-short market; good talent may well have other offers coming in, so you must seize the opportunity. They will make their decision based on how you communicate with them: the speed and professionalism of your response, and whether this response reflects what they have learned about the business from their research and from the interview.

One final piece of advice is to never settle for second best. There is often pressure to fill a role quickly, and as such it can be tempting to compromise and give an offer to a candidate who is 80% right for the job. But just think about this for a moment. If you are continually making these kinds of compromises then gradually over time your business is becoming a worse and worse version of what it could be. Would you really be happy getting only 80% of the sales or 80% of the quality that you potentially could? Although it can be a little painful in the short term, it's better to wait for that great candidate and avoid making compromises on talent.

RECRUITMENT AGENCIES

Although every business is fishing for talent from the same pool, and although commission is earned by getting higher salaries for their candidates, nonetheless recruitment agencies – when managed properly – can be useful allies in your hunt for talent. You may not always be able to find that passive pool of great candidates, and in that case your main alternative is to work with an agency.

The key to having recruitment agencies help your process rather than hinder it and waste your time is to build great relationships with the right agency. First of all, try to find an agency who shares similar values to yours and who you can build a rapport with. In my experience, having a single agency who really understands your company and what you're looking for is far better than ten agencies who don't. In fact, if an agency is constantly bombarding you with CVs which don't seem to have been checked in depth, it's best to tell them to stop contacting you entirely.

If after a few weeks your single agency hasn't found what you need, you could turn to a couple of backup agencies, who you've also built a relationship with, to see if they can help. And perhaps another couple of agencies a month after that. This second and third tier approach can often work well.

So, how do you build this relationship? The key, once you've found the right agency who would be receptive, is to spend time with them so that they fully understand your ambition, essence, spirit and beliefs, what is important to you, how your business works and how it's going to evolve in the future. Get them to come to you, sit down, talk them through it, and spend some time reviewing CVs together. That way they'll know exactly what kind of candidates you are looking for, and if they're a good agency they will only send you those CVs that are right for the company.

When done right, it means you'll never again have to sit through a painfully long interview with a candidate who is so obviously not right for the business. And it means that the agency works to build your employer brand, selling your business to candidates and bringing in great talent. They know exactly what you offer to your employees, and they know exactly what kind of employees you want. This can be a really productive relationship. You just need to put in the required time and effort to build it up with the right people from the start.

Once this relationship is built it can be very useful to hand all communication with the agency to your HR team (however big or small this may be), so that all CVs go through one point of contact and you as the entrepreneur are freed up from the initial process. Having the HR team accompany you to go through CVs with the agency can be a good way to hand things over. Then you can have a meeting with the agency every six months or so just to keep them up to date on the story of the business, any changes that might have taken place, and to bring them in on any big evolutions that happen. In this way your initial investment of time and effort can be incredibly beneficial in the long term.

If you don't have a full time need for a HR team or professional in your business I would recommend that you bring into your team a firm of HR consultants or a HR Director on Demand to work with. I made great advances in the recruitment of team members and ingraining our ambition, essence, spirit and beliefs into our business when I did this.

RETAINING 90% OF THE TEAM

Alongside a solid recruitment plan and employer brand for building your team it is absolutely essential to have a strategy for retaining and developing the people you hire. There are many ways to do this, and I'll explore the key ones here, including some examples of what I did at Inspire.

However, the first thing to consider with retention is whether you actually want to retain all of your team. Jack Welch, in his book Straight from the Gut, writes that in almost every organisation – if we're brutally honest about it – there is a weakest 10% of the team, and that you should really consider cutting these people out of the business.

This is a pretty controversial statement, and it may not be necessary in every entrepreneurial business. But give it serious thought: are there a handful of individuals in your team who you have to spend a disproportionate amount of time on, who are not performing to the standard of other team members, who's ambition, essence, spirit and beliefs are not aligned with the company's and who may be dragging things down? Ask yourself whether your time would be better spent developing and retaining the other 90% of the team, rather than focusing all your energy on shoring up the weakest 10%. As difficult a decision as this can be, really consider the cost of keeping these people around.

Now, let's look at how to retain that majority of team members who you really do want in your business.

COMMUNICATION

In my opinion good communication is the vital contributor to aiding retention and motivation of the team. However, good communication can be a huge challenge: in order to foster an atmosphere of trust and positivity you have to communicate frequently, effectively, and openly with everyone in your company. If people feel that secrets are being kept from them, water cooler gossip and discontent can begin to creep in; be inclusive, and be honest. However much communication you think is enough, you should probably do more! At least some of this communication should be in person – especially anything particularly important – or if you are a lean startup with a team spread around the country / world then you can use video-conferencing technology to get as close to an in-person experience as possible.

At Inspire, as a result of our rollercoaster journey of scaling up, we developed a five-pronged communication strategy, which you can read below and adapt for your own business.

1. Monday morning stand-up

Every Monday morning we have a short, fairly informal get-together where everyone in the company gathers round and we share the good and the bad of what's happened in the past week, and what the week ahead looks like. It's lead by the directors and senior managers, but is an open forum where anybody in the business can openly communicate and share things if they wish. It's a great regular way to keep face-to-face contact between the senior members of the business and the team at large, and to make sure everyone's on the same page.

These meetings usually only last around ten minutes, and we have a member of the support team taking notes and writing out the key points as bullets, which are then shared so that anyone who wasn't around can see what was discussed.

2. Instant messaging

Email has pretty much become the new snail mail system. Just as letters used to clog up in-trays, now emails clog up inboxes. For quick, informal communication between team members which doesn't need to be recorded we have put in place an instant messaging system so that hundreds fewer emails can be sent and inboxes kept much tidier.

We've also set up a discussion thread on this system for every client, so that quick bits of news and information can be shared to everyone involved in that project on a company-wide basis. It's a really efficient way to get those snippets of information out there quickly.

3. State of the nation

This is something that many businesses do – the twice-yearly big company meeting where the entrepreneur stands up in front of everyone and gives a full rundown of everything that's happened and what hopefully will happen. We used to do the same thing at Inspire, but the response in these meetings, even though we put our all into them, was zero. For us the point was to generate feedback, engagement and debate, but we realised that it was simply too daunting an environment for people to feel they could contribute – too many people and too formal.

As a result we changed tack. We still hold these meetings every six months, and it's still a presentation of what's going on in the business, but now we hold four separate meetings in more of a discussion style, breaking the team down into four smaller groups. And these are not divided by department – rather we have a few people from each internal group, so that each has a nice cross-section of the company.

Now we get great engagement and feedback, and have had some illuminating discussions and learned invaluable lessons from these meetings – lessons we would never have learned through a more traditional, whole-company meeting.

4. Have fun

As an entrepreneurial business you should always be thinking about how to do things differently. Communication can be dry and dull, to the point where people stop listening. At Inspire we decided to inject some fun into things. We had a member of the team who was very passionate about videography and keen to use his talents, so we began a humorous monthly video blog which is based around a different theme within the business every time. It features a rundown of the news in the company including funny things that have happened that month.

It's gone down really well, and is a bit different but still shares useful information for the team. You don't have to use this particular idea, but try to be innovative and create fun in the business and in your communication methodologies.

5. Don't shy away from key issues

Many business owners seem to be scared of sharing the long-term aims, goals and ambitions for their company, perhaps because they don't want to raise expectations in case these things don't work out. But from our experience, sharing these goals gives the team focus, ambition, motivation, and an incentive to stay. If the future is one big unknown then all the team has to focus on is their day-to-day work, which is usually much less inspiring than the big picture.

This brings us onto the final point. Don't shy away from communication, especially when it's about something difficult and important. And if it is something difficult and important, then do it face to face. It's so easy to retreat to email to try to avoid confrontation when there is bad or difficult news to share, but your rule should be to share everything – the good, the bad and the ugly – in person. This builds trust with your team, it shows that you actually care, and it ensures that you keep the lines of communication open.

Entrepreneurial businesses are usually small enough that you can do a quick get-together of everyone in the business, or you can walk around pod by pod talking to each team. People really appreciate this personal touch – it could well be a big part of the reason they chose to work for a smaller business. In this way you can see their reactions and respond appropriately. If people receive bad news by email they may well shut down and not say what they have to say to you; rather they'll say it behind your back to other team members with growing resentment. Being able to respond in that moment when the news is received allows you to give your team confidence and reassurance, explain why this has happened, what you are going to do about it, and that in the end things are going to be ok.

REWARDS AND RECOGNITION

Another aspect of the strategy for retaining your team is rewards and recognition. As I already mentioned in the Recruitment section, it can be very difficult as a smaller entrepreneurial business to compete on salary. You must try to be creative within your budget to give your team benefits that they actually want so they stay happy and motivated to work with you. Salary still has to be competitive of course, but rarely will you be able to pay more than a big corporate.

Entrepreneurial businesses can be flexible, agile, and think differently. This means you can literally ask the team what they want in a survey, and respond directly to the requests that people make. This is so much better than simply assuming what people will want and potentially wasting money on a reward that nobody uses.

Many business owners are afraid of asking because they think they won't be able to afford what the team want. But I strongly recommend being brave and taking the plunge. The key here is to have a budget in mind, to be honest about what this survey will mean, to follow-up on your word by implementing immediately the popular requests that you can afford right now, and to create a rollout plan for the future for any other reasonable requests made as the company and budget grow. Also remember that the cost of a strong benefits package will be more than offset by retaining staff for longer: having to go through the recruitment process frequently, with the risk of employing the wrong person, and with periods where roles are unfilled, can be very expensive for your business.

Communicate this effectively to the team with a roadmap of when other benefits are likely to come in and there you have it: you have established rewards that people are happy with right now, and have given the team the promise of further benefits in the future. Everyone will start to recognise that they are getting more than just a salary with your company. Of course you may occasionally get some really out-there, expensive suggestions, but as long as you communicate openly about your budget and the fact these are just not realistic, the team will understand. This is a really great way to keep people on board.

At Inspire we conducted an anonymous survey asking what benefits the team felt were missing, and what – in an ideal future world – they would love to see as part of the rewards package. We set up a box for the surveys and left it in the kitchen for two weeks. We promised to come back to the team quickly after reviewing the results. Clearly the team understood that we were trusting them and seeking their honest view, and so the response we got was phenomenal.

One thing we learned was that several people were requesting benefits that we already offered. Clearly we weren't communicating our existing rewards package effectively enough to new team members. This often seems to be a problem for businesses, where people simply don't know what is available to them. We immediately added information about this to our induction sessions for new starters, which meant many people felt that the benefits package improved instantly, with absolutely no cost to us!

Some examples of the 'quick wins' that we were able to achieve from the survey responses were putting fruit bowls out, getting better tea and coffee in the kitchens, and giving people their birthday off as an extra day's holiday. These were very low-cost, outside-the-box thinking requests that we could put in place within a couple of weeks, and that would make a lot of people in the team happy. They differentiate us from the competition, have become part of our employer brand to attract new talent, and are part of our unique selling point to attract talent.

There were other ideas which were also great but which we couldn't afford immediately; things we could aspire to put in place in a year or so. For all the other ideas that we really liked, we prioritised them against our likely future budget, drew up a diagram of when we expected to be able to bring them in, and then in small groups we went through the plan in detail. The visual communication of the plan makes it very clear, which was important as we wanted everyone in the team to understand it from the start.

We were very honest about what we could afford, what we liked and what was going to happen, and the team loved it. There were only a couple of ideas from the whole survey which we couldn't aspire to bring in, and we explained very clearly and openly why that was. Every year after that we have revisited the programme, communicating clearly with the team and ensuring that people still want the same things, and are happy with the rollout plan. We are also now able to mention during the recruitment / interview process that we asked our team members what they wanted and we delivered it, which is a strong endorsement of how much we care about our people.

The diagram overleaf shows how at Inspire we set out and communicate our rewards and recognition strategy.

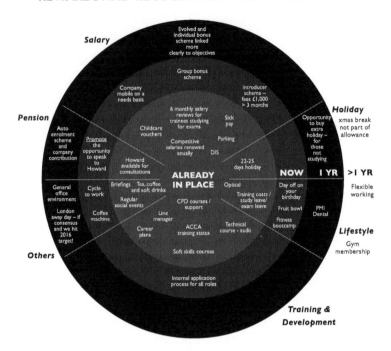

There are many books and theories about team engagement, but I would argue that the reason this approach works is self-explanatory. Team members might well love their work, finding it interesting and challenging, but they must also feel compensated and recognised. By asking your people what they want and communicating effectively how you're going to deliver it to them, you will ensure that their engagement is sky-high and that they remain with your business for a very long time.

APPRAISALS AND TRAINING

Following on from rewards and recognition comes the appraisal process. Every company ought to have one of these, not just as a box-checking exercise but to really get a sense of how every team member feels about their place in the business, how motivated they feel, and as an opportunity to give them the praise they deserve. It's also essential to ensure they are continuing to develop and grow. All too often in the corporate world appraisals are meaningless, dreaded by both the manager and the appraisee and considered to be a waste of time. But with a robust and well-thought out process that's applied consistently to everyone across the business, they can be an incredibly useful tool in keeping retention high in your team.

As with all things, as an entrepreneurial business you have the chance to put your own unique spin on appraisals. At Inspire we realised that the most important thing we wanted to understand and address were the motivations of our team members. As a result, we utilised a third-party tool called 'motivational maps'. This lets the appraisee measure their levels of motivation in their role and also describe what things motivate them in general. Then in the appraisal we can have a meaningful discussion around their answers, and look at what we can do to better align their motivations with what they are doing.

This is especially useful given that people's motivations often change over time: for example junior team members are often excited to learn, grow and develop their career, whereas those members who have just started a family are probably more concerned about money, and eventually their focus returns to career development. If you can understand where somebody is at in their life then you can more easily adjust their goals, their targets, what special projects they are working on etc. so that they are at their best when they come to work.

Think about what would be really useful to learn in your business from the appraisal process, and introduce that into the process. On top of that, introduce standard good practices for appraisals: make sure they happen in a safe space so that everyone can be honest and open; ensure you listen to the appraisee, switch everything else off and focus on them; follow up on what is said in the meeting so that they trust that it is a process worth doing and continue to be invested in making it productive; give credit where credit is due. These are not ground-breaking ideas, but if all of them are implemented together, and are not simply being carried out 'because they must be', appraisals can be fantastic.

Going hand in hand with appraisals are career plans. At Inspire we do these with everyone in the business for the next three years. Career plans do not necessarily mean that in three years' time they must plan to be in a different role: they are more focused on what good would look like for that employee in that timeframe. What can they learn and develop in their current role, and also perhaps where might they like to move to or be promoted to? Having these plans and updating them with every appraisal means that no team member feels stuck or is left wondering what's next for them. Everyone has the opportunity to discuss where they want to go and how they want to develop in the future.

Finally, to help your team with their development, you should be providing ongoing training and development opportunities. Although external courses can be valuable, with entrepreneurial businesses you have the opportunity to really establish your uniqueness by delivering your own very specific and targeted training. First hold in your mind exactly what differentiates you from your competitors, and then work out how best you can instil this into the team via training.

At Inspire we really feel that it is really important our team understand our clients and the entrepreneurial journey they're on, which allows us to empathise and help them appropriately. As a result, we developed an internal business academy for our team to be able to truly understand what it is like to be an entrepreneur, to get inside the heads of our clients and to be able to deliver our service at an even higher level. This academy is open to anyone in the business, and we encourage people to attend. We hold sessions where real entrepreneurs come in to tell us their stories, of both successes and challenges, and share their ambitions, drive and motivations. On more than one occasion we've had to shut the office down for a few hours because everyone in the business wanted to attend. More than anything, this academy has really helped everyone to keep in mind who they are serving when trying to deliver client delight.

All of this means that we are providing training that no other company offers, because it is so specific to our unique selling point. And if you can provide something that your talent cannot get anywhere else, then naturally your retention will be much higher.

What unique training could you provide that is in line with your ambition and essence?

LEADERSHIP

So what is leadership? Let's look now at some of the principles for being a leader.

In simple terms the main difference between management and leadership is that the leader should be setting the direction and ambition of the business – what good will look like in three to five years – communicating that direction effectively, and following up to ensure it is being adhered to. Managers, on the other hand, are rolling their sleeves up, getting involved and specifically directing individuals in a way that will realise the leader's overall plan: they take the big picture and break it down into actual tasks to deliver at the operational level. Getting buy-in from management, then, is clearly very important, which is why communication is such a big part of the leader's role. Once you have buy-in and the management team are very motivated, keeping them up to date on how the journey is progressing will allow them to adjust their management strategy as necessary to keep the business moving in the right direction.

So how does a leader evolve their strategic view? The most important element of this is awareness; being aware of opportunities to seize and threats to avoid. Being aware of what is happening both in the business and in the market will enable you to plot a steady course to fulfil your longer-term goals and ambitions. This means spending time talking to team members and to clients; as well as spending time reading about what's going on in your sphere around the world, and looking over your business's financials in detail, etc.

Imagine the leader is sitting at the centre of a wheel, with spokes running out in all directions bringing in information that enables them to make the best possible decisions for the business. This is the ideal you're working towards. In a perfect world this is what they would spend all their time doing, keeping that strategic viewpoint. There's an old saying in business that the leader should work 'on' the business, not 'in' the business; it's what every business model proposes. However, for most entrepreneurial businesses in particular, this ideal is almost never possible. The entrepreneur also has to work 'in' the business for it to function, because the team is small and because there is so much operational work to be done to actually move forward.

The principle, then, rather than the model, is that the leader should try to gain perspective and be strategically minded as much as possible. Yes, it's often necessary to dive in and work on the operational side of the business. But make sure you block out a morning every couple of weeks – or however often you can spare – to sit at the centre of that wheel and take in as much information as you can. In the days leading up to this time away make a note whenever you think of something that you'd like to spend more time researching, or when you have an idea that could use development. Then go offsite and bring up your list of notes. Research new trends and developments. Plan ahead. Come up with creative new ideas. Set the direction of the business. Decide how best to communicate your plan. Follow up to ensure that you are moving in the right direction.

As you consider your leadership of your team, and how you interact and communicate with each other, I would also recommend that you use some tools to establish what your preferred communication, management and leadership styles are. There are many tools available, and you will certainly be able to find one that is useful for you. The two that I use in my business are Motivational Maps and the Performance Climate System.

I suggest that you do some research, find the right tool for you, and engage with the right organisations to implement those tools effectively in your business.

MARKETING BASICS

With marketing it's hard to beat the old model of the four Ps: Product, Price, Place and Promotion. This is a proven model, and it would be great for you to pause, learn about and implement it in your business. However, this book isn't about teaching you the theories behind marketing – the purpose here is for you to stop and think about how you can improve the marketing in your business in an entrpreneurial way. My experience suggests that marketing in this type of business needs to be highly customer / client centric, rather than rigidly sticking to just the four Ps model.

So what exactly does this entail? It means thinking about and focusing on your customers' requirements. To get started, answer these questions honestly:

- Does your business offer and satisfy its client and customer needs?

- Is fulfilling those needs sustainable?

- Do you have systems and processes in place that can help fulfil those needs sustainably?

You should also stop and think about what it is about your business – and the products and services you deliver – that your customers love. Are there customers who would be willing to tell their story through testimonials, or do you have case studies showing success? How does your business add value to its customers, and how could it add more? You could define this as what your customers want vs what they actually need.

As part of this process you might also want to consider what it is about your business that your clients just about tolerate, and what you could do about it – this way marketing can feed into your wider approach and help you improve your business and customer experience.

Next you must consider what makes up your brand: does your brand actually reflect your ambition, essence, spirit and beliefs? Are those also represented visually? Does it evoke an emotional response in your customers? Consider what makes a great brand in your industry: what brands do you like, and why? You also need to consider your personal brand as an entrepreneur, and what you need to be in order to be successful – how does this personal brand relate to the business, and is it authentic? Is your messaging and marketing consistent across all channels – internal, external, online and offline? Having consistency is vital.

Finally, having a marketing strategy with return on investment checkpoints built in is essential for an entrepreneurial business. You must be able to determine whether your marketing investments are paying off. This might seem obvious, but many people throw cash and resources at marketing without ever tracking the results, and in an entrepreneurial business cash and resources are limited. Having those checkpoints in your strategy will mean you can do more of the things that work and less of the things that don't.

While this section is far from comprehensive when it comes to marketing – and there are many more resources out there which can help you – hopefully you can now stop and reflect on how you can more effectively market your business to prospective and current clients.

FINANCIAL PRINCIPLES

As an accountancy business, Inspire of course has a strong focus on the financials. But this is not just because we enjoy it so much: financial principles are essential for a successful business, yet they are where many entrepreneurs stumble, either because they don't understand them or because they don't want to. The problem is, as anyone who has run a business when cash flow is tight will know, financials can become an overwhelming distraction. One of the biggest challenges can be trying to juggle your money to meet the pressure of paying the VAT bill, the quarterly rent, or funding the extra working capital required for growth. And when your focus is entirely on the money, you will inevitably begin to drift towards the valley of despair.

To avoid this, you must have your funding and financials in good order. Here are five principles to help you achieve a solid financial footing.

1. CASH FLOW

If you want to try to achieve scale in your business, the four key restraints are going to be infrastructure, people, technology, and cash. But the one which most often kills a business's ability to scale is cash flow.

For businesses who have found themselves in the valley of despair, trapped, unable to scale and constantly short on cash, it's essential to go back to your ambition, essence, spirit and beliefs. But this alone won't be enough, you also need to reassess the basics of your financial model. Map out how cash is generated and spent in the business, and work out what it's going to take to add 10% to sales; as well as what cash you need and in what timeline. You need to start from a place of understanding to be able to fix the issues. Solutions could include encouraging clients to pay you more promptly, moving them to a direct debit, or asking for additional funding from the bank if that is what's required to alleviate the problem.

What entrepreneurs often don't seem to understand is that there is a difference between the business model and cash flow. An entrepreneur who has never hit the valley of despair, who fully understands their business model and their route to market, who is thinking innovatively and staying ahead of the market, may nonetheless fall into serious problems by failing to understand the impact their model has on their cash flow. They may appear to own a very successful business, growing fast with lots of clients; but if they don't understand that with that growth comes greater cash needs, they will inevitably fall short. I have often seen businesses fail because they have overtraded, grown beyond their working capital and ended up in an insolvent position.

Make sure that your business model lines up with your cash model. Work out what drives cash in your business, do all you can to accelerate cash generation, and most importantly understand where there is going to be cash shortfall – whether that is from growth of the business or from some kind of seasonal dip. Once you understand this, you must source funding to plug that gap and continue scaling.

2. MEANINGFUL INFORMATION – KPIS

Far too often when I come to help a business I ask for their KPIs, and what I receive is an extremely basic profit and loss sheet – sometimes only including the total for the year to date with no comparative for the previous year. What exactly does this data tell us? Nothing useful: only that the business either did or didn't make money. For KPIs to be of value, they must show useful information that can be used to make informed decisions, not raw data with no interpretation; this is essentially meaningless.

What exactly should KPIs cover? While this may vary from business to business, and industry to industry, the principle is always the same: what are all the different elements in your company driving your profitability? For almost every business this will mean generating leads, converting those leads into sales, delivering the promised service or product, and customer service throughout. There may be other sectors which you feel contribute to the profit margin rising or falling, and if that is the case then you should certainly include those in your KPIs. All entrepreneurial businesses are unique; so take the time to think carefully about this to ensure you capture all the key areas of the business.

By breaking down the information into all these separate sectors, you gain visibility of what is happening in your business now, and what you can expect to happen in the future. For example, perhaps your marketing (say free seminars) in the first quarter of the year failed to attract as many leads as you expected; in that case, sales will inevitably be lower in the second quarter, leading to reduced profits. Without this breakdown of information that details the performance of your marketing efforts, you would be unable to predict the dip in profit, possibly leading to cash flow problems at that point, and you would be unlikely to know why the dip had happened. By contrast, good KPIs in this situation would have allowed you to review the marketing strategy from the first quarter and improve it in future, and would have enabled you to prepare for the anticipated dip in cash flow in the second quarter much more effectively.

Looking at the past can be useful when developing KPIs, especially when looking at trends in the business to see how different sectors are performing and growing. But remember that their principal aim is to help you understand what is going on in your business at present, and therefore what will be coming down the pipeline in the future. What will your cash flow situation look like over the next 12 months, and what can you do to improve it? They should give you the information you need to be proactive, rather than reactive, allowing you to improve your business and help it scale sustainably.

One really vital point about the presentation of KPIs: it has to be understandable and actionable. It needs to be turned into useful information. This means that rather than sending enormous spreadsheets around the company, you should design a dashboard with all the key indicators presented clearly and effectively, using colour as needed and showing trends over time. For example, rather than simply showing number of sales, you display it in red if the number is 'bad', or green if it's 'good', and you include a simple graph charting the number of sales per month for the past year, which will identify trends. This gives a fast and clear snapshot of how a particular area of your business is performing. I describe it as you needing information, not data!

I've mentioned this time and again, but as an entrepreneur with a business that you want to scale, you must learn to let go and trust others in the team to handle the business. However, to do that you need real and specific information which shows what is working and what is not. High-quality, forward-looking KPIs will enable you to stop putting on your Superman or Wonder Woman outfit, take a step back, and see that your team are driving things in the right direction – or to see where changes need to be made so that you can intervene in an appropriate manner.

Finally, if you were ever to hit a rough patch and had to convince the bank or your funding partner to loan you more money, being able to show them these KPIs which indicate exactly where your problems lie, and which allow you to come up with a specific plan to rectify the situation, will make them much more likely to hand over further funding. It will give them the confidence that you know what you're doing and are still heading in the right direction, despite the setback.

3. RELATIONSHIP WITH YOUR FUNDING PROVIDERS

Often entrepreneurs only ever talk to their bank or funding provider when they need money. But this is a mistake: this can be one of the most critical relationships that an entrepreneur has. Don't hold them at arm's length; bring them into the thick of things, let them know about your joys, successes and challenges in the business. This will develop trust and give them peace of mind that there won't be unexpected surprises from you. A strong relationship like this can make a real difference to your ability to secure funding in the future.

4. FORECAST SHORT AND LONGER-TERM CASH FLOW

The fourth principle is that you should be monitoring financial performance against the plan. Using your KPIs to measure against your budget you can see if you are going in the right direction, or are going off track, and you will be able to forecast short and longer-term cash flow. As we saw from the first principle, cash is king, particularly when scaling. You need to predict peaks and troughs, allowing you to foresee the funding that's needed before it becomes critical. This is when having a solid relationship with your funding provider comes into play. Share the forecast with them. Share the expectations of where and when funding will be needed. With no surprises, funding will be easier to obtain in the times you need it.

5. FUNDING OPTIONS

The final principle is a newer one, which has only really begun to apply in more recent years. After the financial crisis of 2008 there were many changes in the business world. The initial years of the crash were tough. As a result, we have witnessed growth in the diversity of funding options for entrepreneurial businesses. There are now crowdfunding sites, peer-to-peer funders, challenger banks, niche asset funders, business angel networks, and even some local council authorities providing funding to newer businesses.

The options are becoming endless, and you must fully understand your funding requirements and how best to combine any number of these sources so that you can get the support you need. It's only by properly taking advantage of these many choices that entrepreneurial businesses will get the growth funding they require.

CLIENT DELIGHT

Whilst many of us are busy ensuring that our businesses are run efficiently, that we're nurturing our team and that they are feeling valued, we should also be questioning what we can do to provide true client delight. This means showing love to our clients and customers, and if you stop and reflect you'll realise that there is always more that can be done to put a smile on their face, and to make the business more client-centric.

Often client delight lies in the little things; those small acts of kindness that make an ordinary service extraordinary, that will give you great testimonials, and that your competitors are not doing. They do not need to be grand gestures. They're the moments when people in your business stop what they're doing and take time specifically to make the client happy.

It is the ability to act impulsively and instinctively by giving your team the scope to do so is what can distinguish an entrepreneurial business from all its competition.

How can you improve client delight in your business? How can you give your team the freedom to delight your clients?

A great starting point when working towards a culture of client delight is to undertake a client survey. Understand what your clients really want from you, what they value, what they would like you to do differently, etc. My own experience has demonstrated that this is an invaluable process and we have instigated regular NPS ('Net Promoter Score') surveys. We have engaged an external third party to undertake this NPS survey. It is really simple. Your NPS score is calculated based on responses to a single question: *How likely is it that you would recommend our company/product/service to a friend or colleague?* The scoring for this answer is based on a scale of 0 to 10.

Those who respond with a score of 9 to 10 are called Promoters, therefore more likely to remain loyal customers and also more likely to provide you with referrals. Those who respond with a score of 0 to 6 are called Detractors, and as such less likely to be loyal to you and make postive referrals. Responses of 7 and 8, which you may consider a reasonable score, are called Passives and ignored in the calculation. The NPS is calculated by subtracting the percentage of customers who are Detractors from the percentage of customers who are Promoters. What has also proved valuable to us and provided really meaningful insights is the follow up question "Why did you give that score?".

CONCLUSION

This chapter was packed with a lot of detailed information, so congratulations on making it to the end! You should now have a good understanding of the fundamental principles for building, retaining and leading a stellar team, and of the financial principles necessary to keep your business running and growing smoothly. Always try to keep in mind what makes you unique, and adapt these principles to fit your own business. Only you know how best to do this.

CHAPTER KEY QUESTIONS
AND EXERCISES

Key questions and exercises that you should consider from this chapter are:

- Determine your perfect future team.

- Are you playing to your strengths?

- Review and improve your recruitment process.

- Who are your least performing 10%?

- How can you improve communication in the business?

- Give all team members a career plan.

- What unique training could you apply?

- Undertake a rewards and recognition survey.

- What KPIs drive your business?

- What is the cash cycle in your business?

- Dont make compromises on hiring talent.

- Undertake a client survey.

CHAPTER 5

The Future

And so here we are, the final stage of this book. You've now examined and explored your own personal passions and values, and so have determined what the ambition, essence, spirit and beliefs of your business should be; you know how to refocus and reposition your business as needed to avoid the valley of despair; you now understand how important personal development is, and how it should relate to these beliefs; and you have learned the fundamental principles of success which you can adapt as needed for your own unique business model. Now it's time to look towards the future of your business.

Essentially this means freeing up more of your time as the entrepreneur to work on the growth of the business, being forward thinking, and ensuring that you are future-proofing the company by working out how to continue generating value. This chapter will look at all these themes in more detail.

FREEING UP THE ENTREPRENEUR

One of the most important things for a business to grow and move forward into the future is that its leader has the space and time to actually lead. You must reach a point where your energy, enthusiasm, focus, passion and belief can be maintained at a consistent level, or ideally where it is growing day on day, month on month, year on year. Where you feel you are able to really spend your time and energy focused on the future and driving your business towards it. You are the heart of the business, and leaders who bring these qualities to work every day will allow the company to shine.

So how to go about this? It's following everything I've already discussed in this book: ensuring the business fundamentals are in place; that you've built the right team around you who you can delegate to. This is what will enable you to focus on the aspects of the business that you enjoy and which keep you engaged. Your engagement in the business, and leading it in an entrepreneurial fashion, is the foundation for future success.

FUTURE-PROOFING

For those of you who found yourselves in the valley of despair, repositioning and realigning your business will not have been an easy process. Even for those of you who avoided it, you will have worked hard and struggled to get out of the startup phase to where you are today. What we want to ensure, then, is that you are always one step ahead of the curve and are making things easier for yourselves in the future. This means future-proofing the business.

FORWARD-LOOKING

The first step in future-proofing your business is to be forward-looking, always trying to anticipate the future. We are now operating in a global world, in a state of constant evolution, with fairly drastic changes in technology coming every few years. Looking only at what is happening right now is a losing bet.

You must keep your eyes open to what is happening and what is coming down the pipeline in your industry, in your local economy, and in the global economy at large. Take the time to really reflect on how these will affect you and your business, and come up with new strategies or with potential solutions for any problems you might foresee. Technology is disrupting and commoditising all industries and you need to be aware of how it's changing yours. If not you will become another Kodak, Blockbuster or Toys R Us; the list of examples is endless.

You may think that your industry is immune to this disruption, but even in a profession such as accountancy the market has been revolutionised by technology. This is one of the reasons why Inspire has developed and evolved its service offering and considered what it is that an entrepreneur wants, which is advice about where they are on their journey – the traditional accounting services, such as bookkeeping, reduction of year-end accounts and calculation of tax liability, are all being commoditised by technology. There are now easy-to-use software solutions and platforms emerging in the market that are replacing the need for traditional accounting.

So if a staid and simple profession such as accountancy can be disrupted, so can any industry: take the time now to consider what is disrupting or could disrupt yours.

VALUE CREATION

All businesses need to generate value, whether that is part of an exit strategy for the entrepreneur, to hand the business to the next generation, or to simply build a legacy and leave it in the hands of the management team. Value creates resilience for the business going forward, so that it can withstand the pushes and pulls that the market will throw at it.

How do you create real value? How do businesses become worth more than just a multiple of their earnings? Let's look at what in my opinion are five key considerations for building value in today's age.

1. Be disruptive to your industry

Being disruptive to your industry means that you are on the front foot, thinking differently and leading the charge towards the future. If you are doing this consistently and successfully you will quickly stand out from the crowd, which generates value. Businesses which only try to follow trends – or worse still try to hang on to a world that no longer exists in which they used to be successful – may generate revenue, but they won't stand out, won't build a strong brand for themselves, and so will not generate much value. I'd go so far as to say that they won't even exist in future!

Stop and reflect on the disruptions that you can think of happening right now in different industries. Some prominent examples include:

- Amazon
- Tesla
- Airbnb
- Uber
- Netflix

These are all significant new companies that have emerged over the last decade which have transformed their industries, and which in some cases have eradicated well-established historic competition.

However, there are also companies out there doing simple disruptive things: an owner-managed business may not always be the huge unicorn which takes over an industry, but it can still be a disruptor. An example of this is Brewdog, whose development and portrayal of their brand in a way that is totally different to any other alcoholic beverage company has been disruptive. Looking at their story we realise that they've also raised funds for their entrepreneurial journey in a different way to most in their industry, which has allowed them to grow, succeed and disrupt. A second example is the clothing company Patagonia, who don't really try to sell to their customer, but instead try to fulfill their customers' and clients' requirements. Take a look in more detail at both of these companies, and then try to think of smaller-scale ways that you can be disruptive to your own industry.

2. Intellectual property

Although many people don't realise it, every business has intellectual property (IP). The traditional definition of IP, which many people still believe to be true, revolves around trademarks, patents and so on – something more tangible, product-based. But you don't have to be a manufacturer to own the rights to something: service businesses, for example, still have processes, ways of thinking, specific uses of technology, brands. These are what makes your business stand out, and it's absolutely essential that they are documented and, wherever possible, protected. They are truly valuable assets.

By documenting what makes your business different and unique, what makes it successful, you are able to easily show the value that your business holds. It also makes it more difficult for anyone to take your ideas and pass them off as their own, since you have a record of them and, ideally, protection.

3. Recurring revenues

The third path to value creation is to have a secure income stream and recurring revenues. Any business that can show it has money continually coming in and repeat customers is guaranteed to be worth more than a business that is only as successful as its last sale.

Whatever your industry, whatever stage your business is at, I would always encourage you to think carefully about how secure your income stream is, and how to obtain recurring revenues. This will be easier in some industries than others; in accountancy for example recurring income is the model, it's fairly easy to achieve this. In some product and service industries it could be more difficult, but I've seen it done. Tying major customers into long-term contracts is an important goal to try and achieve – it builds real value into the business.

4. Subscription businesses

Once you've established a recurring revenue stream, the next objective should be turning that recurring revenue into a subscription model. Just reflect on how you and your business are now engaging with many services and buying many products. You'll be surprised at how many of those new engagements and interactions mean that you're now subscribing for many products and services. Changing a business from a traditional 'invoice / get paid' model to a subscription model can be extremely challenging, and you'll need to seek some advice about how you can go about this.

The subscription model is the model of the future. I predict going forward that the 'invoice / get paid' model will be all but eradicated for all industries and businesses. If we go back and look at the disruptive businesses above, we can see that all of them, in some shape or form, have a subscription model.

So why is this? It's because the subscription-based income stream becomes certain. And in the short term, the valuations being made on subscription-based businesses are considerably greater. Reflect on how you could evolve your business to enable it to adopt a subscription model in the future.

5. That little bit of sizzle

The final point on value creation that I have seen work extraordinarily well is that, although it is vitally important that you have the fundamentals of your business operating efficiently such that you have solid foundations, you also need an element of 'sizzle'.

This means you should always be looking for that next opportunity, that next market to crack, the next product or service evolution that's going to happen. This doesn't mean that you invest all your time and energy into it, but are simply always putting a chip or two out of your large pile on a new exciting gamble. It's these small 'sizzle' bets which allow you to disrupt your industry, and which give you as an entrepreneur the freedom to be a little creative and have some excitement. This creativity and excitement alone is of great value, because it keeps you engaged.

Consider what could be the next piece of sizzle in your business – what small opportunity outside of the normal running of things could you look at, which excites you, and which could potentially create great things for the business. Many of these sizzle ideas may not work out, but that's not the point: they're low investment with potentially high reward. And as such they are bound, over time, to add value to the business.

STRATEGIES FOR GROWTH

When considering the future, and how you may grow as a business, the well-known and widely used Ansoff growth matrix will be useful to familiarise yourself with. This shows how growth can be achieved within four categories: existing markets with current products (market penetration), existing products in new markets (market development), existing markets with new products (product development), or new markets with new products (diversification). Let's look at these four categories now.

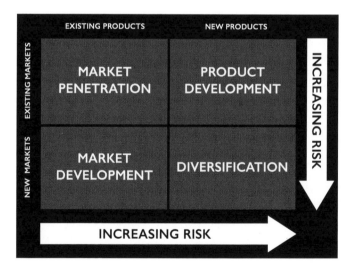

MARKET PENETRATION

Simply put, market penetration consists of selling more of the same products in your existing market. This is about growing your existing markets and getting your current customers to consider more of your products and a wider diversity of your existing product range. It means creating new accounts in your existing market and devoting time, effort and your marketing spend to that market alone. It is the generally accepted 'standard way' to grow a business, and is the method with the least risk attached.

MARKET DEVELOPMENT

Market development consists of selling your existing products to new markets. New markets could be taking your products to a new demographic of buyers in the same country, or expanding geographically. With the world becoming a smaller place, many businesses are looking at market expansion and how they could export their products abroad. In my experience, this comes with a considerable marketing and sales cost, but is actually low risk in terms of not needing to develop new products or services.

PRODUCT DEVELOPMENT

We all have products and services that we market to our clients, but a way to grow your business is to develop new products or services and sell those to your existing market. This comes with the risk of product or service development, but if you can neatly diversify your offering and develop your services, the fact that you've got an existing client base can take some risk away from this approach: you already have a list of people who like what your company provides that you can try to sell to.

DIVERSIFICATION

In this final growth strategy, the plan is that you both develop new products or services, and sell them to an entirely new market. This is highly risky, given the double unknowns of how your new offerings will be taken and how the new markets will work, but if successful can lead to exponential growth.

Which growth strategy you adopt will depend on your attitude to risk; each of the four options above has its own risk / reward level, and you must consider what is best for your particular company and market. However, there are also composite strategies which mean that you operate in multiple boxes at once: sometimes these are the best way to mitigate risk. These can include:

- Strategic partnerships
- Joint ventures
- Company acquisition
- Franchising the business
- Developing new sales channels, i.e. the internet.

THE BENEFIT OF VALUE CREATION ON EXIT

For many entrepreneurs, the goal of value creation is to exit and sell the business successfully. Because while it's possible to get a buyer excited by talking passionately about the virtues of the business, so much so that they would be willing to pay a premium, at some point they are going to do their due diligence, look under the surface and see what the business's true value actually is.

What they will be looking for is that you have secure income streams, that these are consistent and repeatable, and that there is something unique in the DNA of your business – your documented and protected IP – which they can firmly grasp hold of and easily replicate should they take over the business, so that they can continue achieving similar results. They will also want to see that the operational side of things is well-documented and firmly in place, and isn't relying on the entrepreneur to keep things running smoothly, so that it doesn't fall apart as soon as the handover takes place.

If you can show that all of this is in place then the buyer will be happy to pay that premium price. If, however, they look beneath the surface of the business and see that in fact it's only the entrepreneur who is driving the value for the business, that there are no tangible assets in place without the entrepreneur, then they will flee the deal rapidly. There's no true value for them in the business itself.

What would they see if they lifted the hood on your business right now? Where needs immediate improvement in your business? These are great questions to ask yourself to give you an insight into areas that require immediate attention and development.

I often say and I am a great believer that for many entrepreneurs selling the business is not the end goal. Instead the focus could be on passing the business to the next generation, letting the management team run the business thereby securing a passive income, etc. But what I would say is this: the approach and methodology and steps needed to create such businesses are the same as creating a great business for exit.

CONCLUSION

Ensuring that you set aside enough time to look at the future is absolutely essential to keep your business ahead of the competition and to work out your long-term plan. Avoid frantic success, getting bogged down in the operational side of the here-and-now, so that you can lift your head above the parapet and see what's really going on in your market and in your business. Then, by following the advice in the value creation section, you can boost the worth of your business, whatever your future strategy.

CHAPTER KEY QUESTIONS AND EXERCISES

Key questions and exercises that you should consider from this chapter are:

- Are you in a position to free yourself from the day to day? If not, what do you need to do to make it happen?

- How is technology disrupting your industry?

- What's your 'sizzle'?

- What's your business's IP? Is it documented and protected?

- Can you build recurring revenues or obtain long-term contracts?

- What's your strategy for growth?

Conclusion

I hope that, having read this book, you now fully understand where you are on your entrepreneurial journey. Are you in the startup phase? Or are you in the early intuitive phase? Are you approaching the danger zone? And are you in the valley of despair right now, or could you be soon? If so, you should now be able to think of ways and means to reinvent or rejuvenate yourself and the business so that you reach maturity and the good times that we all wish for in business. Finally, you should be able to look towards the future with confidence and with a solid plan for how to move forward.

What you have read in this book is not academic theory; it's based on lessons I have learned, experiences I have had, and entrepreneurial stories I have witnessed.

When I took steps to leave the corporate world and start over, to start Inspire, I had a very clear, personal passion and focus. With this came a strong purpose and quickly a strong culture of hard work and belief in the company that emerged at Inspire. As a result we grew year on year by over 25%.

Yet I did not know I was heading for the valley of despair, and that we were having frantic success. We lost our focus and, worse still, we lost our way. We started to forget where we came from, and as a consequence we began to believe our own hype.

Then came the wake-up call. I realized that while we were having lots of success, I was not having fun. The team were not enjoying it. I was making short-term decisions to relieve short-term pressure and was coming home relieved. I was living what I thought was the dream, but it soon turned into a nightmare. I was in the valley of despair.

It took some courage, but I put a pause on growth, giving me essential time to breathe. I implemented the actions and principles that have been outlined in this book. I made some really tough decisions to ensure we were better placed for the longer term. I realized that I was an integral part of the business and that I was not in balance, throwing everything off. I got help to ensure that I also focused on myself, and got to a point where I could help and encourage the team, and be creative again for the benefit of the business. Then we stepped out into the world, bringing our new inspiration and focus to other entrepreneurs to help them achieve success.

If I could go back to those early days of Inspire, what would I tell myself? I would say this: don't ever stop believing. Have courage in your convictions. Don't get overconfident and believe in your own hype. Don't get distracted; just focus and get on with it. Think about the future, take action, and take it now. This book aims to give the same advice to you.

If you do want to learn more about the principles outlined in this book and also become part of an exclusive entrepreneurial community, go to **evolvemembers.com**

About
the Author

Warren Munson is the Founder of the award-winning tax and business advisory firm, Inspire, and creator of the exclusive membership community for ambitious entrepreneurs and business leaders, Evolve.

With his passion firmly grounded in supporting and encouraging entrepreneurship, in 2004 Warren made the bold decision to turn down a partnership at a major international accountancy firm to set up Inspire – a unique advisory offering focused on a niche audience of ambitious entrepreneurs. A successful corporate career beckoned but, to his colleagues' amazement, Warren chose his passion and made the leap.

Like many fledgling entrepreneurs, Warren started off on his own with just a desk, laptop and phone, but, with grit and determination, the business grew rapidly and is now a multi-award winning firm and Warren an innovative industry leader.

True to his own entrepreneurial spirit, Warren recognised that despite the unprecedented success of his tax and business advisory firm, he had a burning ambition to support an even wider audience of business leaders – to effectively rally together a broader, nationwide network of likeminded individuals so that they can realise their personal and business ambitions in an environment of shared learning, exploration and evolution.

This, alongside his many years' experience in the industry, is what inspired him to write this book and, consequently, launch the exclusive membership community, Evolve (www.evolvemembers.com).

Passionate about balancing personal wellbeing with professional success, Warren spends precious time with his wife and two daughters, and often spends his Saturday mornings cycling long distances across the south of England. A keen charity supporter, he's taken part in several charity cycle rides across Europe with fellow entrepreneurs, and is Chair of Julia's House Children's Hospice.

17666620R00070

Printed in Great Britain
by Amazon